REMEMBERING Singalong Jubilee

ERNEST J. DICK

Formac Publishing Company Limited
Halifax, Nova Scotia

Copyright © Text 2004 Ernest J. Dick

All rights reserved. No part of this book may be reproduced or transmitted in any form or by any means, electronic or mechanical, including photocopying, or by any information storage or retrieval system, without permission in writing from the publisher.

Formac Publishing Company Limited acknowledges the support of the Cultural Affairs Section, Nova Scotia Department of Tourism and Culture. We acknowledge the financial support of the Government of Canada through the Book Publishing Industry Development Program (BPIDP) for our publishing activities.

We acknowledge the support of the Canadian Council for the Arts for our publishing program.

Illustration sources and credits
Canadian Broadcasting Corporation: Jarvis Photographic Studios Halifax, 41 (b/r), 55(t), 77 (t); Martin Fulton/ Halifax Photo Service, 83; Maurice Crosby, 36 (t); McLeod and Lee Photography Toronto, 77 (b); Paul Smith Photography, 60; Robert C Ragsdale Photography Ltd., 20, 21(r), 85; photographer not identified: 6, 9, 11, 13, 16, 17 (t), 20 (l & r), 24 (l & r), 24, 25, 26, 27 (t), 28, 30, 31, 33, 36 (b), 37 (t), 38 (both), 39 (both), 40 (both), 44 (both), 45 (t), 47 (both), 48 (t), 49 (t), 50 (both), 51, 53 (b), 54 (both), 55 (b), 56 (t), 57, 59, 61, 62 (all), 63 (t), 65 (both), 67, 68, 70, 71, 71, 72 (all) 73, 74, 75, 76 (both), 79, 80, 82, 84, 86 (all), 87, 89 (both), 90, 91, 93 (t).

Other Sources: Bill Gilliland, (Two of three albums that jump started the music industry in the Atlantic provinces — the debut albums from The Singalong Jubilee Singers, Catherine McKinnon and Anne Murray) 56, 83, also 82; Georges Hebert, 18 (all), 21 (l), 23 (l & r) , 29, 41 (l / t&b), 43 (b), 44 (t), 45 (b), 46 (l & r), 48 (b), 52 (t), 53 (t), 63 (b), 64 (both), 69, 78, 81, 87, 92 (both); Bill Langstroth, 4, 42; Manny Pittson, 3, 7, 8, 12, 14, 15, 17 (b) (photo Georges Hebert), 27 (b), 32, 34, 35, 37 (b), 58; Garth Proude, 18, 19, 49 (b); 52 (b), 93 (r).
Abbreviations: (l) left, (r) right, (t) top, (b) below

Library and Archives Canada Cataloguing in Publication

Dick, Ernest J.
    Remembering Singalong Jubilee / Ernest J. Dick.

Includes index.
ISBN 0-88780-642-2

    1. Singalong Jubilee (Television program) 2. Musicians--
Canada--Biography. I. Title.

PN1992.8.M87S215 2004   791.45'72   C2004-904415-X

Formac Publishing Company Limited
5502 Atlantic Street
Halifax, Nova Scotia B3H 1G4
www.formac.ca

Printed and bound in Canada

TABLE OF CONTENTS

PREFACE 5

INTRODUCTION 7

1 FROM PILOT TO NETWORK 9

2 FROM 'HALIFAX SOUND' TO MUSIC VIDEO 25

3 THE MUSICAL FAMILY 41

4 THE SHOW'S FOUNDATIONS 57

5 TOO GOOD TO LAST 73

PROFILES AND CREDITS 85

INDEX 95

Singalong Jubilee *cast on location at Uniacke House.*

PREFACE

This book could have been written by Manny Pittson, and in many ways it is his book. Manny, in fact, has written his private memoir, parts of which are included here. His endorsement opened doors and established a credibility I could never have earned otherwise. He has made all of his photos, clippings and files freely available. He corrected errors and gently pointed me in useful directions. He offered his recollections at all stages and comments on all drafts. Manny Pittson encouraged me throughout the book's preparation, demonstrating the kind of mentorship that he showed to so many performers on *Singalong Jubilee*.

This is also the book of all the people involved with *Singalong Jubilee* during its 13-year run. It is compiled from interviews conducted in 2004 as well as excerpts from archives, both print and television. Everyone was generous in their collaboration, and many offered personal photos and mementoes. I trust that the liberties I have taken in transcribing and editing recollections are forgivable. I hope that I have their details correct in the profiles and credits. Some who warranted a profile I was not able to find.

This book would not have been possible without two retrospective series, *Jubilee Years* and *Then Again*, broadcast on the CBC in the 1990s. *Jubilee Years* was a 44-part series made by Manny Pittson and Bill Langstroth and was a fond look back at both *Don Messer's Jubilee* and *Singalong Jubilee*. Re-watching *Jubilee Years* was a wonderful reminder of CBC Halifax's accomplishments in those years. *Then Again*, made by Geoff D'Eon for CBC Halifax, looked at the way performance on CBC Television in Halifax, in the fifties and sixties, stimulated and inspired performance in Atlantic Canada today.

Once again, it was a great delight to work with archive and library friends and colleagues at the CBC, at National Archives and Library, and at the Nova Scotia Archives and Records Management Services. Thank you to Lynda Barnett, Rosemary Bergeron, Leone Earle, Richard Green, Doug Kirby and Barry Smith. In his research and his book, *A Picture by Christmas*, Bill Harper, the unofficial historian of CBC Television in Halifax, provided a larger context for broadcasting originating at CBC Halifax. The CBC Pensioners in the Maritimes were indispensable in identifying all who worked on the show. Glen Sarty made available his unpublished memoir, "As Good as it Got."

Friends and family deserve thanks for their patience and indulgence. Chris Bird transcribed all *Jubilee Years'* references to *Singalong*. He waded through many drafts, made many valuable suggestions and did the initial visual research. John Kirby made his collection of *Singalong* albums available and shared his formidable music experience. My wife Nancy introduced me to the charms of Nova Scotia some 35 years ago. We watched *Singalong Jubilee* together on our black and white television in our first Ottawa apartment. She has been my best friend and strongest ally in everything, including *Remembering Singalong Jubilee*.

Also, I want to acknowledge Jim Lorimer and Elizabeth Eve at Formac Publishing. It was Jim and Elizabeth's belief that the time was now right to tell the story of *Singalong Jubilee* that made this book possible.

All the material collected for this book, including all the interviews, will be deposited at the Gorsebrook Research Institute at Saint Mary's University, Halifax, for those who may want to read the memoirs and clippings or listen to the recollections. It will become part of the Moving Images of Nova Scotia project begun by the institute's director, Colin Howell, when I came to him with the notion of teaching at Saint Mary's University back in 1997, and we shaped a course on the Moving Images of Nova Scotia for the Atlantic Canada Studies Program.

This book has been compiled from private and published sources, as well as from the memories of those involved with *Singalong Jubilee*. Memory is not necessarily precise or completely factual, though it is often insightful and moving. It is invariably selective, both consciously and unconsciously. This is a virtue, not a limitation. Contradictions and inconsistencies remain and offer insight into the different players in the story and their varying perspectives. Readers can decide for themselves.

The wonderful spirit of *Singalong Jubilee* infected every phase of researching and preparing this book. It has been as much fun for the author as it was for the performers and crew.

Responsibility for *Remembering Singalong Jubilee* is mine alone. I look forward to corrections, further leads and further memories. My labour of love documenting the moving images of Nova Scotia continues beyond this book.

— Ernest J. Dick
Granville Ferry, Nova Scotia

Bill Langstroth with the Jubilee *chorus and soloists (1961).*

INTRODUCTION

Lorne White and Hal Kempster perform as members of a male quartet during Singalong's *third season.*

Singalong Jubilee aired on the CBC television network from 1961 to 1974 and became more popular and successful than its creators could have imagined. *Singalong* presented the music of Atlantic Canada — old and new — in a straightforward and imaginative way that resonated across Canada. It left lasting memories with its performers and its audience.

The program was produced in Halifax during the first decade of Canadian television and was part of the 'invention' of television. *Singalong* not only improved the sound of music on television, but it also has a legitimate claim to having originated the music video. It may even surprise the cast and crew of the program to learn how innovative they truly were.

Singalong Jubilee introduced Anne Murray, Catherine McKinnon, Gene MacLellan, Shirley Eikhard, Ken Tobias, and dozens of other singers and songwriters to a national television audience, and launched their careers as international performers. It provided further experience and television exposure for Edith Butler, John Allan Cameron, Harry Hibbs and many more as guest performers from week to week. Finally, *Singalong* made the likes of regulars, Bill Langstroth, Jim Bennet, Patrician Anne McKinnon, Fred McKenna, Clary Croft, Penny McAuley and Karen Oxley known across the country.

The most enduring legacy of *Singalong Jubilee* is undoubtedly its songs. They have become part of Canada's musical heritage. *Farewell to Nova Scotia, Snowbird* and *Put Your Hand in the Hand* have taken on lives way beyond *Singalong*. Dozens of other songs were first heard on *Singalong*, or written by those encouraged and inspired by *Singalong*. *Just Bidin' My Time, The Call, Face In the Mirror, Thorn in My Shoe* and many others written by Gene MacLellan — most while he was at *Singalong* — have been recorded by many other artists.

Shirley Eikhard has now written more than 300 songs, and it all began with *Singalong* and Anne Murray's version of *It Takes Time*. Ken Tobias had international hits with *Stay Awhile, Every Bit of Love,* and *I Just Want to Make Music*. Then there are dozens of others, from Robbie MacNeill and his *Robbie's Song for Jesus*, to Steve Rhymer, to Audrey Alexander and her success with the duo *Audrey and Alex*, to Jim Bennet's flights of the imagination.

Farewell to Nova Scotia, the song that became the anthem of Nova Scotia in the 1970s and 1980s, was discovered by Manny Pittson and Catherine McKinnon

REMEMBERING SINGALONG JUBILEE

among the songs that had been gathered by Helen Creighton, the great collector of Maritime folklore and folk music. It remains the song that Catherine McKinnon has to sing in every performance she ever gives.

❖

Manny Pittson: The folk song was upon us. Those of us who would never have considered listening to a folk song started listening with a new set of ears. I had bought out, of my curiosity, albums of songs collected by Helen Creighton, pre-dating *Singalong*. We found numbers such as *Nova Scotia Farewell*, as the show's theme.

Catherine McKinnon: I came in with *Farewell to Nova Scotia*. Manny said to me, "You can't sing that because it is a man's song." About three weeks later, one of the tunes was not gelling, so Manny said, "What about that Nova Scotia song?" I looked at him and said, "I can't sing that song, it's a man's song." He looked at me and said, "You will sing that song."

So I sang the song, and when it aired the switchboard lit up and I got something like 5,000 letters. It was like an avalanche for us. In a 13-week series, we did the song for a second time. Then at the beginning of the second season we closed our first show with *Farewell to Nova Scotia* and segued into *This Land is Your Land*. It became my signature song.

The rest is history.

The Singalong *cast of 1967. Back row (left to right): Michael Stanbury, Toni Hollet, Hal Kempster, Patrician Anne McKinnon, Vern Moulton, Ken Tobias, Anne Murray, Lorne White. Front (left to right): Jim Bennet, Bill Langstroth, Fred McKenna, Catherine McKinnon, Karen Oxley, Marg Ashcroft.*

1

FROM PILOT TO NETWORK

Singalong Jubilee grew out of the pilot *Folksong Jubilee*, produced by Bill Langstroth in December 1960 and hosted by Pete Seeger, a folksinger best known for his protest songs. The CBC network accepted this pilot as a summer replacement for *Don Messer's Jubilee* from CBC Halifax, but politics prevented Seeger from leaving the United States. His ties to the Communist party and his campaign to combine folk music and labour organizing led to him being blacklisted.

Glen Sarty: Pete Seeger was a regular visitor. Pete arrived every year with his banjo slung over his shoulder to appear

Bill Langstroth with banjo, accompanied by regular Singalong *singers and guests.*

REMEMBERING SINGALONG JUBILEE

on television, do a concert in a local auditorium and tape a 'singalong' for radio. The radio format was simple: a collection of friends, wives, kids, whoever fell into the net, sat on the studio floor while Pete led them in song. Some of the stuff was quite sophisticated but he brought it off, dividing the group into sections and coaching them in their particular parts, then bringing them all together for what turned out to be impressive choral work.

I usually produced Pete's radio recording sessions. In an evening, we would roll tape and an hour later have three impressive 20-minute programs 'in-the-can' ready to run on *AM Chronicle*.

Kent MacDonald: I was among a few others dragooned to be fashioned into a singing group by Pete. I was impressed with the way he could get a bunch singing like larks or bluejays. When the subject came up that we needed a summer replacement for *Messer*, I suggested maybe we could get Pete Seeger to come and do a program like *Singalong with Mitch Miller*. That's how it started. Honest to God! From then on, I had nought to do with it except what fell into my job specs.

Bill Langstroth: It was my hearing on Max Ferguson's radio show a guy named Pete Seeger play the banjo that got me very excited about that kind of approach to music. *Singalong* came out of that folk connection, that folk interest on my part and other peoples' parts.

Glen Sarty: I was looking forward to the *Singalong* summer series. I felt Seeger really did not need to be elaborately produced. We considered adding occasional guests to enhance the show and give each individual program a focus, along with someone of similar stature for Pete to relate to. But, on the whole, I assumed a collection of amateur singers would make the best setting for the show. We could shoot it 'in the round' with the chorus or, rather, audience surrounding Pete and the cameras shooting a full 360 degrees.

Beginning in 1957 and produced in CBC Halifax's brand new studios, *Don Messer's Jubilee* was Canadian television's first hit — to the consternation of both television programmers and critics. The show's fiddlers and square dancers were said to be 'amateurish' and a 'national laughing stock' by the critics, who had great fun at the show's expense. Yet, *Don Messer* rose so high in the ratings that by November, 1961, it was actually ahead of *Saturday Night Hockey* and the *Ed Sullivan Show*.

Although *Don Messer* was successful, *Singalong* was determined to be a good deal more hip. The local production team — led by Bill Langstroth, who had been the original producer of the *Messer Show* — was made up of bright young people who considered *Messer* alright for their parents, but *Singalong* was something they could fashion for themselves and their generation. Despite continuing the name *Jubilee* (which to this day Manny Pittson considers unfortunate), the same timeslot and the sponsorship of Massey Ferguson (which was joined in 1961 by Colgate-Palmolive), *Singalong Jubilee* quickly developed its own identity.

Glen Sarty: The sponsor wanted *Messer* on the air all year round, but he (Don Messer) insisted on a three-month break. Messer was dead set on touring the Prairie provinces, where his most loyal fans and largest potential income lay, and he was not to be deterred. At the time, Mitch Miller was releasing LP after LP in the *Sing Along With Mitch* series. So I simply called Pete and asked if he might be interested in a summer series called *Sing Along With Seeger* – a format identical to the one we had used on radio. He thought it was a reasonable idea and I submitted it through channels leading to the sponsor, who gave it a 'Go.'

Bill Langstroth: In order to keep the *Don Messer* time slot, Fred Brickenden, then the Program Director, and Mr. Syd Kennedy both fought like tigers to get that slot filled by us. I don't think that they have ever been properly credited, but those two men were very proud of their Maritime heritage and their Maritime television station. They very much

10

FROM PILOT TO NETWORK

wanted us in the national picture. We were happy to provide the program if we could make it work. We were all very keen, very bright-eyed and bushy-tailed.

❖

When Pete Seeger proved unavailable for the series, the show had no 'star' or even recognizable talent to draw an audience. The producers had to search out whoever was available.

❖

Jack O'Neil: We did the half-hour pilot with Pete Seeger hosting and the Diamond Trio from New Brunswick for the network to look at. CBC was looking for an alternate show to be competitive with *Sing Along With Mitch* in the States, which was becoming a really big hit, and the CBC had nothing comparable to it on the air. We were all devoted fans of Pete Seeger — he was the king of folk music.

Toronto was very happy with the show, and Bill and I thought we had a winner with this one. Then, lo and behold, within about a week our pilot went out the window. We were devastated. We had the success of the century — we thought.

Singalong stars, September 1963. Back row: Jim Bennet (guitar), Bill Langstroth (bass) and Catherine McKinnon. Front row: Marilyn Davies, Fred McKenna (guitar) and Don Burke (banjo).

Glen Sarty: During the season I got an apologetic call from Pete saying he had been cited by the House Un-American Activities Committee for his alleged Communist connections. As he didn't know what they had in store for him, he doubted it would be fair to me to continue preparing the series when, as he put it, "I may be in jail by then." I accepted Pete's resignation with as much grace as I could muster, expressed my regrets and rushed off to Fred 'Brick' Brickenden's office with the disappointing news.

Manny Pittson: Pete Seeger had signed a contract with CBC Halifax to write and host a 13-week summer series based on his repertoire when, unexpectedly, the House of Un-American Activities prevailed on the US government to call in Seeger's passport. In practical terms, this meant he couldn't travel abroad so that those of us who were involved with his show had to find a substitute series quickly.

It never occurred to me to seek a more detailed explanation of Seeger's predicament. I just assumed that annoyance with his left-wing politicising, which went back for years, had finally landed him in hot water. In those days, we weren't inclined to ask as many questions as we do now. There was still a whiff of McCarthyism in the air on both sides of the border.

More to the point, I was preoccupied with the responsibility of mounting a new series quickly. I was 23 years old and had signed my first producer's contract a few months earlier.

Wayne Grigsby: I once asked Pete Seeger about it and he said, "Yes, the CBC really chickened out on that." I had always heard that it was more of an American problem.

Producer Manny Pittson (left) with Chris Adeney (set designer), Louise Degens (script assistant) and Bill Langstroth (1961).

FROM PILOT TO NETWORK

His sense was that the CBC didn't want to ruffle any feathers and bailed on the idea, or hid behind the visa thing — that they could have got him in if they wanted to.

Jack O'Neil: Bill and I had this terrible conundrum. We were sitting in my living room one afternoon commiserating since we had just heard that we had lost Seeger. So I said to Bill, "Why don't we do our own? You play the banjo; you can entertain." And, that's where it started. Bill said, "I wouldn't be any good as a host!" "Certainly you would Bill. You've got a great personality! You're great for that kind of stuff! Your ego is big enough! It doesn't bother you to go on camera!" We talked about it for quite a while, and that's how *Singalong* started. He convinced Toronto that we would do another pilot.

Manny Pittson: We were desperate. But dress Langstroth in a sweater, and with a long-necked banjo, he looks like Seeger. So we asked Fred McKenna along, and some of Langstroth's drinking friends, and whipped up a pilot. It was all done in a tremendous hurry, and the title was picked in a hurry — a rotten one.

Manny Pittson: There was no time to panic, faced as we were with a 'hey kids let's put on a show' situation. Bill Langstroth talked the network brass into letting him fill Pete Seeger's boots and flew off to Toronto to buy a Seeger-style Vega banjo. I became the producer of the new series, hastily dubbed *Singalong Jubilee* — an assignment I would hold with few breaks until the show's demise in 1974.

Staff announcer Jim Bennet, a trained singer with a broad repertoire, was drafted as co–host only after we assured him that under no circumstances was he to be known as anyone's side-kick or as 'the singing announcer.' Bill's 'rumpus room regulars' became the Jubilee Singers. The network office sent us two featured soloists: Elan Stuart, a pert red-headed Scottish folksinger living in Toronto, and Bud Spencer, a moon-faced 'Danny Boy' tenor from BC. The musical anchor of the production was a blind man who played his guitar across his lap. He was a featured performer, accompanist and de facto music

Bud Spencer performing solo on Singalong's *first season.*

director. We wouldn't have made it without Fred McKenna.

Our first air date was July 3, 1961. Maybe it was because viewers were already beginning to get a little tired of the clichés of variety television that they welcomed our haste and inexperience as natural charm. Our studio set, assembled quickly from seaside artefacts, was a change from the inevitable New York City skyline cut-outs. Not for us the host and guest trading banalities while perched on stools. It helped that one of the early attempts at scripted chit-chat was skewered by Elan Stuart who demanded to know, in her inner-city Glasgow accent, "Who wrote this shit?" — a phrase which became the show's mantra, dug out whenever we ran the risk of becoming too self important.

REMEMBERING SINGALONG JUBILEE

❖

Audience support was stronger than anyone expected. One tele-rating, from the summer of 1962, had *Singalong Jubilee* listed as tenth for Canadian viewers, with a 25 percent audience share behind *Ed Sullivan* and *Perry Mason*, but ahead of *Danny Thomas, My Three Sons, Red River Jamboree* and *Father Knows Best*.

The critics were bemused and more charmed by *Singalong* than they expected to be.

> Singalong Jubilee *is the silliest looking show on view but it doesn't sound too bad. The songs are folk songs and on the whole quite enjoyable. The show itself is harmless and can be neatly categorized as another hot weather offering that helps to pass the time.*
> — Herald Magazine

> *CBC has hit a television gold mine in the person of Bill Langstroth: guitarist, singer and host. One of the most personable young people to appear on our screens in a long time, he sets the tone for the whole show. It is a happy show. Everyone seems to be having a whale of a time, and their gaiety is infectious.*
> — Winnipeg Free Press

> *It was with considerable pleasure that last night I watched, for the first time the* Singalong Jubilee. *It was a pleasure to watch a program that moved from beginning to end in an exciting, well-presented and well-produced way. I take it upon myself to act the part of the armchair quarterback. It seems to me that a program produced by CBC in Halifax should contain a little more of the Canadian folk heritage. You people of the East Coast have the richest background of Canadian folk music of perhaps anywhere — except French Canada. And, those of us that live in other parts of the country would readily appreciate seeing and hearing about it on television.*
> Martin Brockner
> — Letter to Manny Pittson

> *CBC Halifax has a way with music on TV. The prime example, of course, is* Don Messer, *who unerringly hit the nation's rhythmic reflexes. And now,* Singalong Jubilee *has returned to prove there are other ways of doing a community TV sing besides Mitch Miller's way. The show is well-paced, easy-going, very well sung, and a pleasant interlude indeed.*
> — Montreal Star

Singalong *stars Bill Langstroth and Jim Bennet perform together (1963).*

FROM PILOT TO NETWORK

Catherine McKinnon.

Singalong Jubilee, summer fill for Don Messer, would appear to be a shoestring budget show consisting, as it does, of a few informally dressed performers sitting or standing, throughout the half-hour, in the same position by something that only barely passes for a rock. The starkness belies the group's ability to turn out some pleasing old-time favourites – songs you might expect to sing at a cookout. At the same time, the script seems pretty rough. It's entirely possible, of course, the budget doesn't permit one.
— Ottawa Citizen

It was very kind of you to send me a tape with two songs on it from my collection of folk music. Catherine McKinnon's voice seems well-suited to this type of song, and she gave the listener that pull toward the sea, which is in the blood of all seafaring folk, combined with the sailor's nostalgia for his homeland.

Another of my favourites is The Cherry Tree Carol. *Here too, I enjoyed her singing, and also the excellent accompaniment. If that was Fred McKenna, will you please tell him this gave me particular pleasure!*
— Helen Creighton. Letter to Manny Pittson

The unpretentious Maritime-produced songfest completed its second season as a summer replacement last night. All summer Bill Langstroth, Elan Stuart, Jim Bennet, Fred McKenna, Bud Spencer and the Jubilee Singers *have contributed to the pleasure of viewers with their lilting songs and ballads. There hasn't been a more enjoyable program on the air, and they'll be missed in the weeks ahead. Let's hope they'll be back on TV regularly next summer, if not sooner.*
— Ottawa Citizen

Bill Langstroth: Catherine McKinnon knocked them out when she first came to our program. She had this interesting timbre, this control, this production of a voice that had us all on our rears. Manny could not believe what we had found. It was freaky. It was wonderful. I can still hear it. It is one of those voices that stays with you.

❖

Some of the performers came to *Singalong* via *Frank's Bandstand*, also produced by Manny Pittson. This was the Halifax-based CBC rock 'n' roll show that was the regular Friday evening contribution to the network's *Music Hop*, the network's daily pre-supper hour show for teenagers from 1964 to 1967. Manny, thus, had an excellent vantage point to determine which of the emerging rock 'n' roll sounds he wanted to bring to *Singalong* as the sixties rolled on.

For many, their first audition for *Singalong* was a major stepping stone in their careers.

REMEMBERING SINGALONG JUBILEE

Bud Spencer and host Jim Bennet accompany soloist Elan Stuart.

❖

Bill Langstroth: I was scared out of my boots. I was pleased to be considered. I had been performing all my life, but thought that this was a little more than I could handle. There is no question that I found it very exciting, very stimulating. I stayed scared for most of the time that *Singalong* was on. There was enough fear in there to keep me on my toes.

Elan Stewart: I started in Vancouver as a pop singer. And then, when I moved to Toronto, Dave Thomas, of *Country Hoedown*, heard me on a radio show and asked me to do a Civil War folk song — a very beautiful one called *Two Brothers*, that met with good critical acclaim. And, all of a sudden, a little 'Fanny Folksinger' was born. Prior to coming to *Singalong Jubilee*, I'd also had quite a bit of experience with *Mariposa Festival, ABC Hootenannies*, and I also did the *Limelighter* specials, and *Highwaymen On Tour*. I mean, all these are names from the past, but still big in folk.

Catherine McKinnon: Four of us came in from the Music Department at Mount Saint Vincent University in May of 1963. We went to Herschorn Hall on the third floor. There were so many people there, it was incredible. I sang *What*

FROM PILOT TO NETWORK

Michael Stanbury would later become Singalong's *musical director.*

Have They Done to the Rain and *Ten Thousand Miles*. When I sang, there was dead silence in the room. Nobody did anything and my immediate thought was that this had been awful. This was a disaster! It was horrible! Then, in the morning, Mr. Pittson called from the CBC and said that I had been accepted as a chorus member and as a soloist. I got off the phone and jumped up and down and screamed blue murder. I was so excited, you could hardly scrape me off the wall. I couldn't believe it.

Marg Ashcroft: I auditioned at Herschorn Hall back in 1963, and it was a great night for me because there were a lot of people, a lot of good singers there. It was a long night, and at the end of the night I was chosen to come back and have a camera audition at CBC. And, after that — it was a couple of days — I got a call from Manny

Pittson. Graham Day was involved, too. Graham came down and auditioned me in the wardrobe room of CBC, and I sang *My Bonny Lies Over The Ocean*. He asked me to sing that and harmonize it. I was so excited!

Michael Stanbury: I first heard *Tom Dooly* by the Kingston Trio coming from a New York radio station on AM radio late at night. I think it was about two weeks after I heard that song that I went out and bought a guitar for 40 dollars, up at North End Stationery, on Agricola Street. You know, the strings were about a half-inch off the neck and a chord chart, and boy, my interest in that kind of music just never stopped.

Karen Oxley: I had just had my sixteenth birthday. I remember very clearly the first year I was on *Singalong* as a regular, and showing up at rehearsal with my *Coles Notes*

Karen Oxley on set during the ninth season.

REMEMBERING SINGALONG JUBILEE

International star Anne Murray made her television début on Singalong Jubilee.

because I was writing exams that year in high school. But, I grew up on the show with all these people. I grew up in front of the nation, really.

I can remember going into class, English class, and having all my *Singalong* lyrics. You know, kind of whipping them off on the side of the desk so that everybody could see them. I must have been totally obnoxious. It's a wonder I had any friends left at all. When you come from a very, very small place, as I do — just a small village in Hants County — it's a pretty heady thing when you're just turning 16 and you're on national television every week. You know, the glamour and the glory of it, it was all there.

Audrey Alexander: I received a letter on April 1, 1964, asking me to audition for *Singalong*. It was a typed note with a hand-drawn map of where to go on Young Street for my audition. I showed my mother the letter and then I tore it up and put it in the trash, as I thought it was a joke being played on me — by a friend — as it was April 1. My mother retrieved it from the garbage and said, "Call on Monday. No one will know that you called if it's not true and if you don't tell anyone." Well, Monday, I did call and found that it was for real and an appointment was made for an audition.

Anne Murray: It was my brother David, he was an intern at the VG in Halifax, and he worked with a nurse [Sylvia Wedderburn] who sang on *Singalong*, and approached her and asked, "How would my sister get an audition?" It was my brother David who started this whole thing. He got an application form and sent it to me.

Bill Langstroth, relaxing on set.

It was 1964. It was my very first plane flight, from UNB in Fredericton down to Halifax to audition. I sat down and auditioned for everyone, I was part of the crew. They threw me in with all the singers and they asked the singers to report on how good I was. I had two friends with me for moral support, from university. I hung around the next day for the auditions for solo positions. I sat on a stool with a hat and a ukulele and sang *O Mary, Don't you Weep, Don't you Mourn.*

That's what stuck in Bill's mind and that's what stuck in Brian Ahern's mind. According to them, Manny Pittson was not interested in having a college kid on the show. I was too 'friggin' nervous to look around at anybody else.

Bill Langstroth: This kid came and sang, and I thought, "Oh God! We have to have her on the show." But, we could not put her on because we had people who had been on for two years who sang alto. All we were auditioning for was the chorus. If somebody came out of the chorus to do a solo once in a while that was part of the evolution.

In the meantime, the members of a CBC television crew working in Fredericton were invited to a party where they heard a voice that turned their heads.

Jack MacAndrew: Anne Murray starts to sing and it is clear that she is one hell of a singer. We set up cameras and record 15 minutes of Anne Murray singing. I took it into one of the editing suites, and she is coming through the camera like you wouldn't believe. I go down the hall and get Langstroth and Pittson. We run the film and Langstroth peers at the screen and says, "Isn't that the one we turned down?" Pittson says, "Yeah, I think so." I say, "Well, fellows, you can turn her down again if you want, but I think she is one hell of a singer."

Sisters Patrician Anne McKinnon and Catherine McKinnon together on set.

Jim Bennet and Bill Langstroth in a publicity photo (1963).

Bill Langstroth: When we went back to Anne and asked her to audition for the next series she said, "No, of course not, I don't want to be turned down again."

Anne Murray: I said, "Not a chance: I am not going back there. That was a horrible experience and then I got turned down. I am not putting myself through that!" I flatly refused! Then he said, "If I promise you that it is just a formality, go through the hoops, but you are going to get on the show, will you come?" I said, "Sure, I'll do that." Anyway my pride had been hurt. But, I did go back and the rest is history.

Singalong Jubilee really was a wonderful place to launch

everybody. It was a great training ground, and there was an awful lot of talent that came out of that show. I don't think anybody ever expected it. It was just one of those things. Timing, I think, is everything. But, it was great. We learned so much doing that show, too.

The McKinnon sisters (1965).

Patrician Anne McKinnon.

Patrician Anne McKinnon: I entered the talent contest in Halifax, at Saint Pat's High with Donny Burke's sister, Betty-Anne. She was playing guitar and I was singing, and we won the contest. The prize was a hundred dollars, which was quite fabulous in those days. And [Bill Langstroth] asked me to come and audition for *Singalong* later that year. And I did, and I was accepted.

Ken Tobias: I met Patrician Anne, who was on *Singalong*, at a hootenanny contest in Dartmouth. And, I had a tape from a show that we had done in New Brunswick — a CBC show, *The Ramblers*. So, I gave her a tape, and she said, "Well, I'll let you know." And I kept calling her, 'cos I had finished high school and I wanted to get the heck out of Saint John. And, she gave it to the producer, Manny Pittson. Next thing you know, I got a call to do *Music Hop*.

Davey Wells: I came out of another television show, *Music Hop*. And when that show finished, I did an audition for *Singalong Jubilee*, and here I am. It's sort of interesting, kind of magical to me that when I became a part of

REMEMBERING SINGALONG JUBILEE

Singalong Jubilee, I got into another aspect with the country, with the folk. I hadn't been doing too much of that up until then. There was a lot of different music that I'd done before I got into *Singalong Jubilee*, like the blues and a little bit of rock and jazz, which I think made me appreciate *Singalong Jubilee* so much.

Garth Proude: I came from Charlottetown, PEI, with a group called the Tremtones. This was back in '64 or '65. I met Brian Ahern, who just happened to come into our dancehall, at the old Roll Away Club (where Don Messer used to play, by the way). He called me back about a month later or so, and said, "Would you like to come to Halifax and join our band?" And, I thought it was just a band at the time. Turned out to be a TV show called *Frank's Bandstand*, and that's where I met Jack Lilly and all the rest of the gang.

Jack Lilly: My brother used to play drums, and he'd sort of leave them lying around, and I got bangin' on 'em, until I got a little bit better. And some of the guys around used to play a little bit, and then we got a little bit of recognition in Halifax. And then, an audition came up for CBC, for *Music Hop*. So, I auditioned with a band called *The Five Sounds* from Halifax, and I got picked out of that. And from that it evolved into *Singalong Jubilee*.

Georges Hébert: Well, my dad was involved with a band in Moncton. I started playing harmonica with my dad, and then, I guess when I first saw a guitar, I said, "That's it, that's what I want to do." And I even ended up playing on a local TV show. They were the Bunkhouse Boys in Moncton. Then that led to the Brunswick Playboys, which was a rock 'n' roll group in Moncton. And that's how we ended up guesting on *Music Hop, Frank's Bandstand*.

(Clockwise from top left): Davey Wells (seated), Penny MacAuley (seated), Garth Proude, Jack Lilly and Georges Hébert.

Robbie MacNeill: It was a wonderful start for me to be on television at that age. It was scary going into a studio when you are not too sure of what you are doing, being on television — sort of like going to school without having your homework done. My involvement with Anne Murray, Ken Tobias and John Allan Cameron all came out of *Singalong*.

Clary Croft: When I was watching it as a teenager, they were the groundbreakers for people like me. There were

Penny MacAuley: *Singalong* was the beginning of my being a grown-up. Clary and I were referred to as the 'gold dust twins,' because we were the youngest on the regular chorus. Because of *Singalong,* I got my first apartment and my first car.

Shirley Eikhard: My family is a musical family, and we were in Prince Edward Island for the summer in 1970. The Prince Edward Lounge was Johnny Reid's place. I wasn't allowed into the bar until after everything was closed down and there was a little hoedown, and I got up and

Penny MacAuley.

the 'Patrician Annes,' who were doing what was considered pretty avant-garde music for the time. I can remember the year that Patrician Anne brought in the song by this unknown guy, and people were saying, "Oh? Interesting song. I guess it'll fit in," and the guy's name was James Taylor. It was pretty heady, for a 19-year-old kid to walk in and the first day you started rehearsing with these people. It was neat.

Shirley Eikhard.

REMEMBERING SINGALONG JUBILEE

sang some songs on the last night that my parents were playing in the bar. Karen was there and she heard me sing, and she said, "Why don't you send me a tape?" I had no clue what she needed it for, or whatever. A few months later, I got a call from Manny Pittson, and he said, "Do you want to be on the show?"

Bill Langstroth: Shirley [Eikhard] was a 15-year-old and had written maybe a half dozen songs by that time. I know that Anne Murray saw them and said, "This kid's got some stuff." She sang on our show when she was a teenager because she had the voice, and she is still one of the finest singers in the country.

Shirley Eikhard performing a solo during one of the show's final seasons.

Key cast members on set (left to right): Jim Bennet, Catherine McKinnon, Bill Langstroth (back), Don Burke (front), Fred McKenna, Michael Stanbury.

2

FROM 'HALIFAX SOUND' TO MUSIC VIDEO

Television was first broadcast in Canada in 1952 in Toronto and Montreal but it took some years for it to reach all major centres in the country. CBHT, the Halifax-based CBC station, went on the air in December 1954, from makeshift studios at the College Street School near the Public Gardens. Purpose-built studios and broadcast facilities at Bell Road were finally ready in October of 1956.

In those first years, television programming was either live from local studios, or brought in on film from other production centres. A series of relay stations across Canada in 1958 began to allow instantaneous cross-Canada broadcasts, but simultaneous network broadcasts, as we think of them today, were very limited in the first two decades.

Shows such as the *Alf Coward Show, Alibi Room, The Sounds of Jazz* and *Reflections* introduced local orchestras and bands to television. *Downeasters* was the original bluegrass show that predated *Don Messer*. *Hi-Society* was a live high school talent show hosted by Jim Bennet that gave dozens their first appearance on television, including *Singalong* regulars Catherine McKinnon, Karen Oxley, Clary Croft and Bennet himself. *Land of Old Songs* was based on the folk songs collected by Helen Creighton and hosted by Ken Homer. Television was going through a technical evolution while *Singalong* was on the air. Videotape had just been invented and Halifax received its video equipment in 1960, earlier than most of the CBC. Tape was used for the first *Singalong* pilot. Colour also came to CBC Halifax in this era, the first program being the *Singalong* cast and crew presenting *Christmas Eve with Catherine* in 1966.

David Carr operating the then state-of-the-art Auricon 1200.

❖

Bill Langstroth: The first shows were done live-to-tape. We had tape that you couldn't stop. You set it going and

REMEMBERING SINGALONG JUBILEE

Christmas 1968. Back row (left to right); Toni Hollett, Vern Moulton, Marg Ashcroft, Ken Tobias, Patrician Anne McKinnon. Front row (left to right): Bill Langstroth, Anne Murray, Fred McKenna.

boom, you had to do the show. It might as well have been live-to-air. One day, just after the second commercial started, I broke one of the strings on the banjo and that had me in an absolute flap for 30 seconds. I don't know how I recovered. That kind of thing did not happen a lot, but there were some scary moments, crazy moments.

Colour first came to Studio One in what they called the Gemini system. Essentially, it was two film cameras mounted to our two video cameras, recording simultaneously on a continuous roll. In other words, you could not cut them back and forth — they were just recording machines picking up whatever that camera was seeing. Roll at the top of the show, there was no going back once we started. Then later, we would go to Toronto with our cans of film and we would put them on tape, mix them on tape back and forth.

Jim Michieli: In the early days with black and white, there was not the intense light. They used to mount two lights on the front of the camera, so that when they dollied into the subject, they often did not have enough light to fill in on the faces. It was always a problem getting enough light on the faces in the close-ups.

Going to colour was a completely different situation because you needed more light. In the black and white days, it was basically pancake or panstick makeup, and you worked in the grey tones to determine whether it was too dark or too light. We were all tested for colour blindness, because you would be useless. We would then use less

FROM 'HALIFAX SOUND' TO MUSIC VIDEO

makeup to achieve a more natural look.

With black and white, you tended to be very heavy-handed because you could shade and highlight to shape the face, as otherwise the face was very flat. But as soon as you did that with colour, the shading under the chin would look very dark, very made up. So all of a sudden you had to become very light-handed and go very natural, almost like street wear makeup.

❖

The sound of *Singalong Jubilee* became very important to the cast and crew, and came to be known as the 'Halifax Sound.'

❖

Manny Pittson: When I first came to CBC in Halifax in 1955, the audio for music shows, for entertainment shows, was done live — a few microphones in front of the orchestra or band, with everything going live-to-air. You had live music pick up and live-to-air. That works fine up to a certain extent, but when you want to get complicated — when you want to do shows that have a lot of pace about them — you had to figure out some way to make things the same way in rehearsal as you want them on the show.

The *Messer* people found that they could record their fiddle numbers or their dance numbers in advance. Then, by playing them back for the performers in the studios and having the performers in the studio lip-synch in time to the tape, they had a degree of creative control over timing and pace, and camera shots, and performer movement and lighting. Television production in those

Top: Bud Spencer and Peggy Mahone with a guest (1961).
Above: Editing tape at the CBC.

Bill Langstroth and the Townsmen.

days, and up until recently, was all about control. The more elements you have under control — that do not change from rehearsal to rehearsal, or from rehearsal to tape — the better off you are. That's the reason they started pre-recording and having performers lip-synch.

A little later it occurred to us — people like Bob Theakston, Brian Ahern and myself — that there must be a way to make things look a little more natural. It was mainly my doing. Why couldn't we have singers sing live over a pre-recorded band and chorus track? You needed highly directional microphones for that kind of manoeuvre and you needed directional speakers. So we started doing band tracks, where the guitar player was standing with the singer, and the guitar player would simply be moving his fingers on a dead guitar because he was already recorded, and the singers were singing live. This made for more of a performance than merely lip-synching.

When we started pre-recording music to be sung live over tape, we realized we could do a lot more with the band track than simply record it onto an audiotape. We could enhance it in a number of ways. We could enhance by doubling the chorus so that instead of 16 singers, you

FROM 'HALIFAX SOUND' TO MUSIC VIDEO

were hearing 32 voices — we would be overdubbing. We were still using mono tape, one-track tape. So you would put down one track and, if it sounded a little thin, you could overdub it.

But lo and behold, the more you overdub, the more tape hiss you get. Two or three dubs and you have had it. We realized that what we needed was multi-track tape recorders, because then you could overdub without hiss. By the time we finished, we were up to four tracks and overdubbing became part of the routine of the show. A lot of this came out of *Frank's Bandstand,* where there was a bit more of an experimental atmosphere. Running both shows, I could take the best ideas from both shows. We even went so far as to create a little logo to represent something called the 'Halifax Sound.' The sound was always top-notch on *Singalong,* with the experimentation coming from *Frank's Bandstand.*

Georges Hébert in studio.

Bob Theakston: We were quite proud of our sound. We always cranked out pretty good stuff. Toronto was always jealous of what we did. We had a standing competition with Toronto, and we could do it better and cheaper than they could. That was always our attitude. We developed what we called the 'Halifax Sound.' It was clean and intense. We had three or four people that really wanted to make the sound good: Brian [Ahern], Georges [Hébert], and Freddie McKenna was there, and his ear was really sharp.

We had a constant argument with CBC Engineering Headquarters in Halifax. We did not like the compressors and companders at the transmitter because they took away the dynamics of the music too much. I was constantly fighting with people in Montreal about the frequency response of the transmission lines and the dynamic response of the facilities we were given. We could record it okay, but then we couldn't get in on the network. By the time we heard our efforts being broadcast, it sounded terrible. We managed to have our local transmitter remove the compander in order to get a little more dynamic width into the music.

Georges Hébert: Bob Theakston was our CBC audio man and he let me handle the dials. He let me mix the show. It wasn't a requirement or anything, but every move that I

Singalong Jubilee *production meeting. (Left to right) Don Jackson, audio; Thomas Matthews, producer trainee from Malaysia; Manny Pittson, producer and director; Bob Smith, production assistant.*

did on a knob or a slider, I had to justify. He would say, "What are you doing there?" And I would say that I am eqing or putting a bit of high end on the vocal. He would say, "Why are you doing that?" I would say that it sounds a little dull and he would say, "Okay, fine," and we would move on.

Garth Proude: We were recording in those days on a four-track format, and so if you made a mistake, the whole group would have to do it all over again. Nowadays, every instrument is on a separate track, so you can just do your own part, or even little sections of it. It's no problem making a mistake now. In those days, everyone had to wait and everyone had to do the whole thing all over again. I was so young and inexperienced that I really had to learn fast.

Milt Isnor: In those days, we didn't have airtight headsets, so whatever the producer said, the performer might be able to hear. So, I had to make sure that I kept my hand on my earphone when I relayed instructions, because they might be cursing this performer for screwing up and you had to tactfully get them to do it again and give a better performance, to get it right this time. Sometimes the

FROM 'HALIFAX SOUND' TO MUSIC VIDEO

Anne Murray recording on location at Greenwood air base (1969).

producer might want another take, and the performer had done his best take. I always found myself on the performer's side. In many cases, I could see their point of view: the fact that the director might have missed the shot he wanted, if the guy gave a great performance that should be sufficient.

❖

Ricky Nelson's *Travelin' Man* in 1961 has long been considered the world's first music video, and a claim is being put forward for *Chantilly Lace* by the Big Bopper from 1958. Equally, *Singalong Jubilee* and Manny Pittson have a legitimate claim to having originated the music video. An anonymous program proposal for *Singalong Jubilee* articulates the idea of the music video before the show went to air.

> *Take the show mobile combining the natural resources of Nova Scotia, good music to sing along with and to listen to, and a little romantic history, fact or fictional, with regards to the various locations we will be at. The*

Catherine McKinnon, Jim Bennet, Anne Murray, Fred McKenna, and Bill Langstroth 'ride the rails'.

show will be made up basically of pre-taped VTR items. Film will also be used, and we will also have live inserts from studio and on location, with a live mike pickup occasionally. We will go from number, to number using the most economical means of VTR editing, either direct splicing or using live studio insert to ensure positive continuity of mood and feeling.

Certainly, it is evident that Manny Pittson had a unique sense of the possibilities of the music video and devised ways to present music on television that no one accomplished before *Singalong*. But, the performers and crew of *Singalong* were equally determined to find new ways to perform on television, even if none were particularly aware that they were inventing anything. They were simply trying to make their presentation as interesting and as much fun as possible, and to transcend the limitations of shooting in the studio.

❖

Manny Pittson: We had to get out of that little tiny studio somehow, didn't we? The Messer show had already devised the technique of using dancers to kind of break up the action. We didn't have that device, so we went outside the studio.

Someone once said, "Manny you must have seen the Soundies," and maybe I did. I don't recall seeing these around Halifax when I was a kid. I discovered them years later when I did a special with Cab Calloway. I do recall taking a shoebox, cutting a square out of the box, and pulling a roll of paper illustrated with my images through it, and calling it television. The song that I illustrated was *Johnny Doughboy Found a Rose in Ireland*. I know that I was eight at the time because I remember where we were living. The problem that I quickly ran into was that you couldn't be literal in your illustration. You didn't have to be literal.

Jack O'Neil: The music video concept started with Manny Pittson and *Singalong* — there was no question about that. It had never been done before. It certainly hadn't been done in Toronto. They just wanted to take the show out of the studio. They wanted to give it variety, so that we were not just sitting around a set looking at each other and singing to each other. Nobody termed it 'music videos' at the time. I don't remember that expression ever being used. We pre-recorded the audio in studio and then, with one camera, we lip-synched the visuals. They were slow processes. By today's standards, they were not even basic. But at the time, they were revolutionary, because they worked.

Manny Pittson: The performers loved to do mobiles [location shoots]. Catherine McKinnon was one of our veterans. She would always be walking along a seacoast lip-synching something to do with a ballad of lost Jimmy Whalen. One day we put her out on a rock, shot her, went to lunch and left her there. The tide came in. It took a man and a boat, and an oar and couple of other things to get her back.

Catherine McKinnon: You might think it was fun, but I remember the day that the crew left me in Peggys Cove with the tide coming in. Five guys had to drop me in by the boulders, and then they looked and went, "Ahh, it's

Nancy deLong, Singalong *soloist during the show's later years.*

break time, bye!" and they left me. They left me there. I was very scared. And, I think I was singing *Fair and Tender Ladies* and praying a lot that I would get through it before I was washed away by the tide.

Patrician Anne McKinnon: Manny had a unique sense of lyric and location. He was a master. There is no question in my mind. I did a song called *There's Somethin' Happenin' Here*, which is a rock song, and Manny, for some reason, chose the dead of winter in a graveyard, the oldest graveyard in the country. He didn't want to have any footprints in the snow, so it was your classic one-take wonder. I had a walkie-talkie under my cape. The crew were freezing. It was forty below, which is not exactly a nice winter day. The setup really took hours, and the end result was fabulous.

Karen Oxley performing at a festival in Tatamagouche.

Bill Langstroth: One thing that never appeared on air was the *Teddy Bear's Picnic*, with Jim as the father, me as the mother, and Karen Oxley as the goldilocks figure in it all, and Bill Grice, one of our graphics people, dressed up as the bear. He came steaming through the picnic, chasing something or other, as the bear, and caught the side of my head and knocked me cold.

Manny Pittson: I think that I got pretty adept at driving down the road and seeing scenery out of the corner of my eye and saying that's where Ken Tobias singing *North Country Fair* will work because it just kind of looks like north country.

We always had songs that were lip-synched — nine times out of ten. Occasionally, we had songs like Gene MacLellan thumbing along the road to the airport, *In the Early Morning Rain*, which weren't lip-synched. I notice today that they are a mix of lip-synch and non lip-synch. In other words, you see the singer singing the song, and sometimes they are just acting a little skit. But, that unreal quality is still there. How many music videos have you seen which purport to be something real going on? They don't. They all are a funny tension between reality and surrealism.

I don't recall any letter ever saying to me, great job on those mobiles. All I started to notice was that after a while more and more of them were on the network. I think we started something new. It's part of our contribution to television, I hope.

Manny Pittson's role in the invention of the music video has even been acknowledged by Moses Znaimer, the founder of MuchMusic. At the Sheridan College Media Arts Awards in April 2000, Znaimer recalled that Manny's combining of interesting pictures with the songs of great performers had come to mind when he was conceiving MuchMusic.

Singalong Jubilee also got out of the studio by taping shows in front of audiences at the Lunenburg Fisheries Exhibition in 1963, moving on to the military bases of the Maritimes in 1964, and to the Confederation Centre in Charlottetown and to St. Paul's Anglican Church in Halifax, both in 1965. These were, by no means, routine outings in the second decade of television. Similarly, live audiences didn't quite know what to make of television in these days.

FROM 'HALIFAX SOUND' TO MUSIC VIDEO

Crowd in Tatamagouche watching a Singalong Jubilee *live performance.*

Staid and venerable St. Paul's Anglican Church in Halifax throbbed with some of the liveliest music in its 216 history one recent Sunday night, and almost everyone agreed, lost none of its dignity. There were complaints after the recent service, too. Some called it 'scandalous.' One person said it was a 'blot on St. Paul's history.' A few irate people phoned a local radio station to protest. But, most of those who complained, were not at the service. Nearly all who were, liked it.

— Weekend Magazine

More than anything, *Singalong* prided itself on the quality and excellence of its music. It was far more than just another hootenanny show, and that is why it survived longer than the usual television variety series. It took its inspiration from the singing traditions of its Nova Scotian location. Freddie McKenna gave it a country sound but never the country and western glitz of Tommy Hunter or Hank Snow. It was also open to the blues and spirituals suggested by Lorne White and the rocking and rolling being heard on *Frank's Bandstand*, which was also being produced by Manny Pittson.

Musical excellence was only one of many ingredients in the show's success. *Singalong*'s professionalism relied on a flow of new ideas, new songs and new performers.

❖

Jack O'Neil: The only similarity between the original pilot with Pete Seeger and with *Singalong Jubilee* was staging the show 'in the round,' and we had never done this before in television in Halifax. Bill said he wanted to put Pete Seeger in the middle. I remember the set: the studio was all black limbo, and a series of granite rocks constructed from Styrofoam, with people sitting on the rocks, and Pete front and centre of this circle, with the Diamond Trio off behind and to the side.

When we began working on the *Singalong* concept we followed through with 'in the round.' Everything we did was brand new, there was no right or wrong. If it worked, congratulations. If it didn't work, then try something else. We were writing the book on broadcasting. You could never make a mistake in television back in those days.

Jim Bennet.

Manny Pittson: By the time the second summer season [1962] was over, it was becoming obvious that natural charm can only take you so far. The hosts were running out of song material. The chorus needed directing. There we were sitting on one of the continent's premier folk song collections and we were still singing of 'dem old cotton fields.' The seaside detritus, out of which we had manufactured a set, was beginning to smell in more ways than one. In short, it was time for *Singalong* to turn pro.

In preparation for the 1963 season, I instituted regular

John Allan Cameron (1968).

FROM 'HALIFAX SOUND' TO MUSIC VIDEO

Above: John Allan Cameron leads the cast in song on Singalong's *1967 Christmas broadcast.*
Right: Bill Langstroth mugging for the camera.

auditions to make sure we were using all qualified local talent before importing 'from away.' We began keeping an ear open for songs written by locals and combed the Creighton collection for folk songs that could be brought to television.

Bill Langstroth: They hauled people in and auditioned them every year. Some of them were great, we kept them on file, we didn't forget them. But, all of that stuff happened as a result of both Manny and me, and Penny Longley, and anybody else who knew anybody coming to us and saying, "Hey, you-know-who is really good." We would go out and hear them, if we could. We would have official auditions in Sydney and Moncton and various other places once a year.

> *There are, of course, several things about* Singalong Jubilee *that lift it out of the level of the suburban do-it-yourself hootenanny and into the realm of professional entertainment. However informally, the songs are arranged, and almost always in a way that makes them easy and pleasant to listen to. And however relaxed, the singers are all better than your average whisky tenor.*
> — *MacLean's*

Don Burke, a member of the original cast, on banjo.

Tom Kelly plays a washtub bass during Jubilee's *12th season.*

> *As the folk idiom was gradually superseded across the country by more complex forms of popular music, the* Singalong *material changed too. The new songs were more demanding than the folk for which* Singalong *was initially designed. "Over the years, the world of popular music grew up," Pittson says, "and our people just grew along with it."*
> — *Nova Scotia Magazine*

Tom Kelly: It had a real singalong banjo folk music feel to it. As the years progressed, music changed, with more of a singer-songwriter approach. And, that's what Manny had in mind when he asked me to come as co-host. To get away from the 'singalong' idea and to get into the singer-songwriter approach brought me there.

FROM 'HALIFAX SOUND' TO MUSIC VIDEO

The Singalong Jubilee *cast (1967).*

❖

The CBC thought it knew what it was doing when it cancelled *Don Messer's Jubilee* in the spring of 1969 and moved *Singalong* from being the summer replacement for *Messer* to full-season, prime-time replacement. The CBC had a new President, George Davidson, who was competently and steadily allowing the CBC to refashion itself into a relevant and 'hip' contemporary medium. It was happy to let Doug Nixon, Entertainment Program Director for CBC Television, "bloody well kill the geriatric fiddlers," as he put it in one of the CBC's more celebrated and ill-considered quotes.

No one anticipated the firestorm of protest that spontaneously broke out across the country — thousands of telegrams and a march on Parliament Hill, led by the Massey Ferguson tractors that the audience of *Don Messer* was so familiar with.

REMEMBERING SINGALONG JUBILEE

Top: Bill leads the cast in song during Singalong's 7th season.
Right: Singalong *album art.*

So, *Singalong Jubilee* began a new life on Friday evenings in the fall of 1969 under a considerable cloud. Nevertheless, the show actually improved slightly on the audience numbers that *Messer* had on CBC-owned stations across the country (1.14 million viewers compared to 1.13 million). Most of the critics were won over easily enough, but one, perhaps, could already see the writing on the wall.

> Singalong Jubilee, *which has been the* Messer *summer replacement since 1961, is only two years fresher, newer and younger than the* Messer *show itself.*
> — Toronto Daily Star

In a few years, *Singalong* itself was axed for being outdated.

3

THE MUSICAL FAMILY

Singalong Jubilee was — and is today — a family. Everyone who worked on the show testifies to this. The unofficial parents of this family were Hal Kempster, who many called 'Poppa' or 'Dad,' and Karen Oxley, who became the den mother. Hal was in his mid-thirties when he joined the *Singalong* chorus in 1963. Karen was younger than most, joining *Singalong* in 1962 at the age of 16. She quickly became both a favourite and a confidant of everyone. Musically and personally, she was much wiser than her years. Both Hal and Karen stayed through to the end of the series in 1974.

❖

Penny MacAuley: It really was a family. I suppose that there are other television shows over the course of history that have been families. Definitely ours was a family, which has continued to this day. Hal Kempster was one of the bass singers in the group — I called him my second dad. When he passed away, I felt like my father had passed away again.

As far as Karen goes, she was like the mother hen. She got us focused, she was full of energy, and had the most incredible sense of humour. She loved to laugh. Karen was a true

Above: Hal Kempster in costume.
Left: Penny MacAuley. Right: Karen Oxley.

41

Performing on location.

professional. She had perfect pitch. Anne always looked to Karen, "Do you think I am singing that right?" And Karen would say, "For god's sake, Anne, you don't need me to tell you what's good." But, Anne always looked to Karen for confirmation that any performance was as good as it could be. Karen imparted a lot of that to us as singers.

Clary Croft: There was such a sense of family, with the producers, with the technicians, with the musicians, with the cast. I came in and found a family, and really, really quickly felt a part of that family. Incredibly nurtured. Never told to do things differently. There would be a hand on your back, it would be Hal Kempster pushing you into the mic a little bit. It would be Patrician Anne looking over and saying, "Lift your chin up so that the tenor part comes across." It's that kind of thing. Karen just took me to her bosom. She became a real mentor, a very, very dear friend. Actually she threw the stag party before I got married.

The family did everything together, even away from the studio.

Catherine McKinnon: We were very close as a group, with the cast and crew. We would meet for breakfast on Quinpool Road at a Greek restaurant, Sophie's. They were wonderful to us. And when we finished the show we would go back up and have lunch there. We would be in the studio at seven-thirty on a Sunday morning. You

THE MUSICAL FAMILY

would have gone to the market to get a shopping bag full of clams, and we would all head out to Lawrencetown Beach. We would fish, and we would swim, we would play Frisbee. We just did stuff together.

Marg Ashcroft: When *Singalong* went to prime time in 1969, we taped the shows at night. We couldn't have the studio until the supper-time show was finished, which was *Gazette*, which ran from six to seven. We would all go in for makeup call, have our hair done and all that, and we would go in and they would set up our set. We would start at eight — I don't remember. Sometimes we would finish on time, and sometimes we would be there until three-thirty or four in the morning. We had such a good time. We were such a close group that we sat and talked and laughed, and smoked so many cigarettes. But when I came home, I would sleep well. I would have enjoyed myself.

Davey Wells: As we worked together for all the years, even today, like we were friends, not only in the studio or on stage, but off stage. We were all so close.

Georges Hébert: The thing with that whole bunch of *Singalong* people — I don't think that I have ever been in a group or a situation, where you really felt like you were a family. There was no friction, there was no one disliking someone else. It was just like one big happy family. It was such a treat being in a situation like that.

We did the show on weekends, with everything being pre-audioed, and no possibility of making a mistake, and they liked everyone to be smiling on the show. We used to go have lunch at the Dresden Arms as a group, and we would always have a couple of beers at lunch. We would come back and everybody would be joking, not drunk, but sort of in a jovial mood. Manny actually liked it because everybody was smiling for the cameras. We all looked like one big happy bunch, which we were. You wouldn't drink on a TV show now. When you are all pre-recorded, you feel like you have done your work, you are just sitting there pretending you are playing.

Catherine MacKinnon.

Tom Kelly.

The *Singalong* family accepted newcomers easily. Tom Kelly knew full well that he was coming to a well-established family when he became host in 1971.

Tom Kelly: If I had been in the place of the people who were watching an outsider come in, I don't think I would have been as gracious about it as they were. I was always welcome.

One time, I came down with the car and we had rehearsals over a music store on Barrington Street. I offered people a ride after rehearsals and we set out to find the car. We were wandering all over half the city, because I could not remember where I left it. I was so embarrassed because here were three or four people tagging along behind me to find the car. At one point I made the mistake of saying, "I am such a mindless turd," and from that point, I officially became "Mindless" — that was the name that everyone used for me.

Anne Murray: It was a lot of fun. It was a great learning experience. Probably the best learning experience. I mean, I knew nothing about television. I got to sing harmony, which I had done some of, but I mean it was so intensive. It was every day, practically. And I learned about lights and cameras and things, so it was a brand new experience for me, and a lot of fun. And, of course, the people were a hoot. It was like a party.

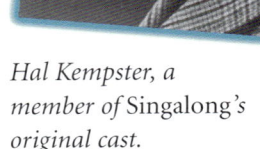

Hal Kempster: Ladies left the show because their husbands were transferred, or their families were growing up. The replacements who came in were often younger, but yet we all still melded together, and it just seemed to me that… I don't know, probably just sheer luck, but it gelled.

Ken Tobias: To this day I thank Manny, and I thank the whole show, because it was the greatest teaching. I learned so much from everybody. Karen Oxley, I mean, just observing her and how professional she was. I learned background vocals, how to do 'em. Today, when I do production and work with my band, it all goes back to *Singalong*. I think about how to build voices, and so on and so forth. It comes from *Singalong*. And I had a chance to do my own songs. Where else could a young guy come on a show and, all of a sudden, they let him do his own songs? That's amazing, it really is amazing.

Tom Kelly: I came to the show as a solo performer, and I had never really worked a lot with other people — developing the songs musically, and then going into the studio and being part of the chorus, adding vocal harmonies. Vocal harmonies, I had never worked with before, I had always been the leader. A lot of aspects of my music were expanded. Everybody was part of the chorus.

Edith Butler: *Singalong Jubilee* was like university. Not only did I learn the technique of television on *Singalong*

Hal Kempster, a member of Singalong's *original cast.*

Edith Butler became a frequent performer during the late 1960s.

THE MUSICAL FAMILY

Jubilee, how to work with the microphone, the cameras, I even learned English. But I also learned a way of life, because *Singalong Jubilee* was really a way of thinking, having a good time expressing your culture, your own individual culture, through songs and music. I learned how to write music with Brian Ahern. I even learned from my mistakes. I remember one time they sat me on a barrel. During the song the barrel broke, and I fell into the barrel, and I had Fred McKenna's guitar, and I broke the guitar. And after that I told myself, "Never will I take myself seriously on a television set because you can always fall in the barrel."

Bill Langstroth.

❖

Laughter on *Singalong* came from many directions. Bill Langstroth's graciousness and good humour sustained the family through many a long rehearsal or taping. Davey Wells' infectious good humour still resonates loudly when watching tapes of the show. Less well known for their sense of humour, beyond the *Singalong* family, were Gene MacLellan and Karen Oxley. And no one was immune to the practical jokes that pervaded everything they did.

❖

Penny McCauley: Davey Wells was a guy with a great love of life, loved to sing, loved to laugh. I remember a lot of laughter.

Anne Murray: Gene was a very quiet guy, very introspective, but he was funny. He had a wicked sense of humour, very dry. He really made us laugh on the set of *Singalong*. He would have us in stitches until Manny was just about crazy. He and Davey Wells were the worst.

Georges Hébert: Gene MacLellan and Davey Wells were a couple of characters, like a couple of bad kids in school at the back of the class. Hard to believe, when you see Gene. On this particular day, Gene was sitting with his guitar at the back of the set,

Davey Wells clowning around on set.

someone else was singing in the front. It was a foreground shot and the camera would slowly pan across the set with the singer in the background, and you could see us in the background, slightly blurry, but you could still make it out.

Karen Oxley and David Wells.

Jim Bennet was the unflappable announcer for *Singalong Jubilee* in the grand old CBC radio tradition that continued what J. Frank Willis and Don Tremaine began. But, *Singalong* also gave voice to Jim Bennet's versifying and song writing when they needed to lighten the mood or fill a hole.

❖

Clary Croft: Jim was the highly-educated, sophisticated, trained baritone voice, very fine songwriter, but then with this acerbic and brilliant wit and puns. Jim's funny songs — his *Black Rum and Blueberry Pie* and *Thanks A Lot For the Teabag* — are a big part of my repertoire. I probably do more Jim Bennet songs in my performances than

So Gene was looking at Davey, and pretended to be picking his nose, and that ended up on camera. Usually, when they shoot a shot, we would go and stand around by a monitor and watch the number. So we all watched it and there's Gene picking his nose. We couldn't believe it, and Manny said, "Yeah that was good." So we were going, "I can't believe that he did not pick that up." It made it to air and everything.

Catherine McKinnon: Karen used to call Anne "Ugger" Murray. They would get on the set and do things, and Karen would laugh so hard that she would cry, and the makeup and mascara would run all down her face. I adored her and I adored her comic gift, which was profound. She had amazing natural comic timing, and she had a great voice, and she was a great music student. She was special.

Milt Isnor: Garth Proude was the bass player, and Garth's wardrobe was a pretty hip wardrobe for the time. Some of those pants were pretty tight fitting. On one occasion you could really see his penis, and someone started singing, "Garth, you'd better hide your lump away." He had to change his stance because his gear was showing. It was all done in fun.

Jim Bennet.

THE MUSICAL FAMILY

anybody else, because they are so definitive of the tongue-in-cheek way that Maritimers look at themselves. People always look at Jim and think, okay, Jim is the serious guy and sings the old ballads — but Jim had this incredible levity that some people didn't see.

Bill Langstroth: When Jim Bennet walked into rehearsal once and said, "Let's try this song *Black Rum and Blueberry Pie*," we were all on the floor, we were laughing so hard. There is just no stopping that song. I have sung that song in the craziest places since, because it is such a wonderful story about what we are supposed to be like here in the Maritime provinces. That was our take on being Maritimers and our take on being singers, musicians and performers. It did speak to that silly idea that here we are, a bunch of rubes who couldn't muster a thought if we were paid to. It's such a wonderful ironic kind of thing – a lovely piece of Jim's work.

Bud Spencer, Elan Stuart, Bill Langstroth and Fred McKenna perform together on an early broadcast.

❖

Fred McKenna was the galvanizing force of the family, but he was challenged with his blindness, with his drinking to excess, with his weight (350 pounds at one point), and with his personal life. Everyone came to help Fred at one time or another, full of admiration and love for his fundamental decency and musical genius.

Fred McKenna solo.

47

REMEMBERING SINGALONG JUBILEE

Bill Langstroth: He had several people that tried and were partially successful at keeping him going while we were doing the shows. I don't think it's any secret he had a drinking problem, and he had a personal problem, a life problem, as most drinkers do. He would be our number one sadness that I recall.

Milt Isnor: He was blind, he drank a little too much. Fred was always afraid of having an accident. One of his fears was that he would get his sight back — he didn't think he could cope. He had coping skills for being blind. Somebody he had heard of had a bump on their head and got their sight back and went crazy because he could not deal with that sort of thing.

❖

In an interview in 1975, Fred McKenna explained that having been born blind and therefore growing up with this condition, he did not have to retrain, as is the case with someone who loses their sight.

Catherine McKinnon: God knows that he loved his beer, and he used to belch like crazy. I remember Trish teaching Fred how to shake his head 'no,' because he would never know how to do that. When you love people very much you become very defensive about them. I was doing a tour by myself across the country in 1968 and, by the time I got across the country, I had been asked so often if Fred drank that, by the time I had finished, he had never had a drop in his life. He always did the show, and always made the show, so what he did in his off hours was none of their business.

Lorne White: The first time that I saw Fred, I was amazed at his capacity to drink. It was the first time that I saw anyone take a quart bottle of ale and empty it. Yet, I doubt that he ever missed an appointment. He was able to play quite well, even inebriated he was still an artist. I always enjoyed driving

Top: Catherine McKinnon (1967).
Above: Karen Oxley (left) and Lorne White (right) on set.

him wherever he had to go. He was always appreciative of anything anyone ever did for him. There were many people who took him under their wing because he needed a lot of help, in transportation mostly. There were many stories of how people would take advantage of him — they would steal from him but they would never take his guitar. They would take his watch or his possessions.

Wayne Grigsby: In his bad days, Fred was pretty much a horror. There are legends of wardrobe people not going anywhere near him, and makeup people not wanting to touch him. He would come in hammered out of his head, he'd been up all night partying and just totally a reprobate. But that was all part of the legend of the show.

Jim Michieli: Fred was a handful. He was great. You couldn't ask for a nicer guy. Very talented. Just unfortunate that he had a weight problem — that was very difficult for the wardrobe department. He would perspire heavily, and you had to keep an eye on his makeup, keep the hair in place. If he started to perspire and get shiny, then it was touch-ups all the time.

Anne Murray with Fred McKenna.

Garth Proude.

Garth Proude: We were travelling up to Greenwood one time to do a gig, and we had to pick [Fred] up — Davey Wells, Jack Lilly, Gene McLellan and myself. Of course he didn't have a suitcase, but he had a garbage bag — that was his suitcase. He said he had a matching bag to go with that — another garbage bag. He carried his booze in there. He was only half-dressed and sitting in the back, and Davey and Gene had to try to get his socks on. Of course he had to have a drink at the same time.

Anne Murray: Freddie would know that if he was lighting up that they would roll tape. He would sit there with his cigarette over his guitar, and his guitar would be covered with ashes – he used to put the ashes in the hole of his guitar. He would feel around with his hand and that's where his ashes went, and the rest were all over the floor because he smoked all the time.

Ken Tobias: Freddie, I loved him. We all took turns taking care of him on the show. He didn't have anyone in his life, so everybody would take him to his home. He couldn't take care of himself very well and he drank quite a bit. One day in the mid-sixties, a woman came into Freddie's life and she was fantastic. Freddie used to come to set and his hair was combed, he was bathed, he was amazing. Everything was taken care of. You couldn't believe how happy everyone was for him. This was true love, and he had actually found someone that knew how to take care of him.

During that season, in the middle of the night that woman died, and he was alone with her and couldn't do anything about it. I remember Freddie came to the taping

Five stars perform on a Christmas broadcast.

Michael Stanbury.

THE MUSICAL FAMILY

Ensemble, Christmas 1968.

of our show, he would not stay at home, he said he had to do the show. I remember him downing a pint of rum and not even fazing him. He would be doing his song and the tears were in his eyes, and he was slapping that guitar (he was a brilliant slap-guitar player). Everyone was looking at him, and we all were smiling, but behind that we had tears in our hearts. It was one of those shows that I will never, never forget.

Wayne Grigsby: Toronto had always been uncomfortable with Fred McKenna. The Head of Variety was always trying to get them to put Fred in the back, or on the side, or put sunglasses on him, or do something. To me, the great glory of *Singalong Jubilee* was Fred McKenna. He was the heart of the show. He was an authentic country performer playing, it seemed like, 112 instruments — and playing them all well. He, for me, kept the show honest. And if you are going to 'futz' with that, then clearly you are 'futzing' with the heart of the show.

I came across an exchange of telexes between Manny and Len Starmer, the Head of Variety for the network. It was all couched very carefully at the beginning, but got stronger and stronger the further into the correspondence they got. It was essentially making the point that we need to hide Fred, with the last one from Starmer saying something to the effect, "Get that grotesque off the air." Manny's response was, "Fuck off, strong letter to follow."

Manny Pittson: I think that I may have prepared that message, but I think that someone along the line refused to pass the telex. I recall sending it, but I suspect that a night manager responsible for internal communications within the CBC refused to send it. But, the story got around in any case.

❖

The family naturally had its marriages, the most prominent being that of drummer Jack Lilly and Karen Oxley in 1966. This was a thoroughly *Singalong* occasion. Patrician Anne McKinnon and Anne Murray were attendants, virtually everybody from cast and crew attended, and the proceedings were shown the next season on an episode of *Singalong Jubilee*.

Karen Oxley (left) and Jack Lilly (below) were married in 1966.

Another marriage was that of Eva Fogarty, a chorus singer for a season, and Milt Isnor, long-time floor director. The relationship that Bill Langstroth and Anne Murray developed in the late sixties, culminating in their marriage in 1975, was quieter and more private for personal and professional reasons, with everyone respecting that.

The *Singalong* family has faced death. Fred McKenna was the first to die, in 1977 at the age of 43. Gordon McMurtry, a chorus member in the early years, was also in his forties when he passed away in 1988. In recent years, Hal Kempster, Davey Wells, and Ted Flynn (another early chorus member) have all passed away.

Patrician Anne McKinnon was diagnosed with Hodgkins disease in 1972. Her cancer was advancing rapidly in the 1973-74 season when she was co-hosting. Her gorgeous long hair, which she was so proud of, was falling out. Jim Michieli, the makeup artist for them all, had to blacken her scalp so that the television lights would not be reflected, and everyone shared in her affliction. Patrician Anne died in 2000. Karen Oxley's multiple sclerosis was not diagnosed until after the series ended, but being another one of the show's teenagers, and being so central to its music and its people, many shared news of her progress until she passed away in 1992 at the age of 46.

When Davey Wells passed away, Lorne White gave the eulogy and his musical partners from *Singalong*, Garth Proude and Georges Hébert, put together a tribute CD of the music they played together. The proceeds paid for Davey's headstone.

When Gene MacLellan took his own life in 1995, the *Singalong* family was not taken completely by surprise. His profound sadness was known to the family, even if no one knew how or why he carried it with him.

❖

Clary Croft: You knew there was a dark side with Gene — a lot of his music reflected that. I never saw that dark side. I always saw a very caring, passionate musician. I think he had some demons, and I frankly think that his music helped him through a lot of it, but obviously it didn't help him enough.

Manny Pittson: For me, the enduring icon of the *Jubilee* years is not Don Messer and his fiddle or Bill Langstroth and his banjo nor is it Marg & Charlie or Anne Murray. It's the wounded face of Gene

Patrician Anne McKinnon.

Karen Oxley (1968).

MacLellan and the eyepatch, which couldn't mask the pain we heard in his songs or the unhappiness that would lead to his tragic death. Gene was one of the last guests to appear on *Don Messer's Jubilee*, just before the show was cancelled in 1969. I heard his high, lonesome sound and immediately hired him as an unofficial writer-in-residence on *Singalong Jubilee*. The years that followed were Gene's most prolific period as a songwriter.

REMEMBERING SINGALONG JUBILEE

Lorne White: We wondered whether Gene was driving when he had his car accident when his father died. We never knew. I never was sure whether he had this thing on his conscience about his dad's death, whether he felt responsible or what. He was burdened. I am sure that he was in love with Karen (Oxley). Hard as I tried, I couldn't help him. He would come here and play his guitar and sing songs and tell us how his songs were inspired by her. He was a troubled, troubled man. Just such a great talent.

Jack MacAndrew (Gene MacLellan's manager): If you listen to the lyrics of MacLellan's songs, so many of them are about finding release. If you listen to the lyrics of *Snowbird, Put Your Hand In the Hand* and many others they all say, "I am unworthy but you can take me by the hand, take me to a better life." It's part of the dark side of the creative spirit. Who knows why God makes us that way?

❖

When the series ended, Patrician Anne McKinnon kept track of everyone's birthdays and children. Anne Murray and Bill Langstroth hosted some memorable reunions at their

Above: Gene MacLellan.
Left: Lorne White.

Malagash cottage. To this day, Penny McAuley hosts summer picnics and Marg Ashcroft organizes potluck suppers, with both keeping telephone lists.

❖

THE MUSICAL FAMILY

Penny McAuley: The family that I developed there is with me today. They are all my extended family. Of all the things that I have done in my varied career, that is the group of people that has lasted from then until now.

Graham Day: Most of the cast, most of the time were unbelievably cooperative. They were lovely people to work with, and a lot of us have kept in touch. It was a happy show. If you have been involved in the music or the theatre business, it's a bit like the church choir — pretty tense at times, with people being difficult. *Singalong* didn't have those characteristics. It was not lovey-dovey all the time, but there were no screaming performers. It was just a very comfortable group of people.

Top: Penny MacAuley.
Above: Cast members on the 'old mill' set.

The Dropouts: Vern Moulton, Karen Oxley and Lorne White.

Vern Moulton: That was my life. I thoroughly enjoyed it. I could hardly wait for rehearsals. We spent hours and hours rehearsing in Lorne's living room, over and over and over again, but loved every minute of it. To be in *Singalong*, it was one big happy family. There was a lot of love for everybody. You didn't care if you even got paid for it. That didn't enter into it at all.

Album cover for the first Singalong Jubilee *record, later re-released on CD.*

4

THE SHOW'S FOUNDATIONS

The undisputed leader and visionary of *Singalong Jubilee* was Manny Pittson. He was in the studio observing the original pilot, *Folksong Jubilee,* and then jumped at the opportunity to become director and producer when Bill Langstroth became the host. He grew with the show, taking a break for the summers of 1967 and 1968. He was convinced to come back when *Singalong* replaced *Don Messer* in 1969 and stayed through the 1972-73 season.

Manny always brought an open mind and an open ear to presenting music on television. He never had a musical vision for what *Singalong* — or any particular show that he worked on — should sound like. But, he recognized authenticity, excellence, and potential in performers and in music.

Manny had an instinct for making television. He was not easily satisfied with what television could do and was constantly challenging it and inviting everyone he worked with to invent new ways to make television. He combined a technological aptitude and curiosity with a respect for the television audience, and listened to what they told him through audience ratings. And, Manny worked well with performers and production crew.

Catherine MacKinnon and Manny Pittson pose on set.

❖

Bill Langstroth: Manny was the producer of that show and the director of that show, and he did it in his own style. And he did it mostly with our enthusiasm because we were getting terrific results. We were having a good time

Catherine McKinnon performing a solo.

with music. Singing was fun and singing was recreation, but we also wanted to reflect some of the artists and some of the people who were around the country, the Canadian performers who were really top performers, or had the potential. It was Manny who took it to the next level.

Wayne Grigsby: Manny was a very smart, acerbic, grounded kind of guy. The cast used to call him the Greek tragedy, because he always seemed to be carrying a black cloud around over his shoulder. He was not a guy that smiled easily. He didn't suffer fools gladly. I found him a very smart, savvy television producer, who had a real sense of the audience, what worked for the show, and what didn't work for the show and how you put it together. If he was a little crisp with people, it was because he didn't want to spend a lot of time debating. He was a guy who just had a terrific sense of how to do a variety show.

Graham Day: Manny has never, never received the recognition that he deserves. Not only did he conceive the show, he conceived each and every segment of the show. He was the guy who identified potential performers. He gambled on people, developed them and brought them along.

Catherine McKinnon — I remember her audition very well — Manny used to say, "Please state your name, your telephone number, what your are going to sing and what key." Catherine said, "The *Jewel Song* from Faust." Manny — God bless him — said, "Okay. It's a very difficult piece to do." So she sang a bit of it. Manny said, "Fine, do you know anything else, do you know any folk music?" She said, "I know one verse of one song, *What Have They Done To the Rain*." He said, "What key?" She said, "I don't know." He said, "You start and Freddie will pick you up," (and he did) and the rest is history. If you weren't Manny and if you weren't open — genuinely open to possibilities — someone like Catherine could have been lost in the margins. That's just one example.

Clary Croft: The first solo I ever did, I was a little bit intimidated by Manny. He's a lovely, lovely man, but I didn't have a lot to do with him. Then a couple of weeks into the season, I was given a solo spot. Manny was the kind of person that would let the artist pick their song. At that time, I was heavily into Kris Kristofferson, and I picked this very depressing moody song off the Kristofferson album.

Here I was, this sensitive 19-year-old guy, and I wanted to show that I knew this other kind of music — that I wasn't just there to sing *Hi Jolly, Heh Jolly*. It was god awful, it really was god awful, and Manny said, "Is that really the song you want as the first solo song going out?" He never said, "Clary, we are not going to do it," and bless him, he let me do it. But then he said, "Here's another song you might want to try," and I did it. I think it was an Irish jig.

When the ratings came in my first solo got pretty low, and this Irish thing went in the high 80s, which was pretty darn good. He showed me that you may have a particular taste in music, but you also have to realize that you have a particular audience out there. He did it so wonderfully, without putting me down.

Shirley Eikhard: It's thanks to Manny that my songwriting was recognized in a big way. Over Christmas of 1970, Manny apparently played a demo tape of new songs I'd

Manny Pittson.

sent him to do on *Singalong* for Anne Murray, who was recording at the time. She heard *It Takes Time* and quickly went into the studio with it. The first time I knew anything about this was by getting a call from Capitol Records, asking me to come up to their Malton, Ontario office and hear something. Believe me, it was a thrill of a lifetime sitting in their office and hearing Anne singing my words and music! She had just come off of her huge hit, *Snowbird*.

Graham Day: I am a great Manny admirer. I thought that Manny was unbelievably talented. There was no such thing as a bad shot with Manny. He blocked (planned) every shot for the show from ground zero. It wasn't like *Messer*, the same shots week after week. Never on *Singalong*. I used to look at some of the work he did, and I used to think, "Wow! You just don't see stuff like that out of Toronto, let alone out of Hollywood."

Wayne Grigsby: He never let the constrictions of shooting a show in Halifax get in his way. We don't have a big studio to do big production numbers? Fine. Give me the mobile, and we will do a big production number out in nature. They found a way to make it interesting, to open up the show. They didn't stand around and say you can't do that on television. I never ever heard that, and I suspect nobody ever heard that. I think that Manny is one of great contributors to the musical life of this country.

Jack O'Neil: Manny fully believed in audience research. He said we have to know how the audience is reacting to the

Anne Murray recording a 'mobile'.

songs, to the performers. That is critical for the success of the show. So, he struck a deal with CBC Toronto that they would do audience research. The show would be on Friday night and by Monday morning on his desk in Halifax would be the research notes on the show. But primarily, Manny was focussing on Anne Murray, because there was a remarkable talent here, but if it is going to be successful, you can't go on a gut reaction or luck alone. So, we knew whether the audience liked Anne Murray wearing blue or green or whatever. Hair styles, the songs she sang, interpretation, whatever. We spent a whole season researching. We created a package around the performer. Never before, certainly in CBC's history, had we ever concentrated on marketing a performer like that, and it certainly worked. It was way ahead of its time, the way the production team went about using audience research.

Manny Pittson: I remember taking note of audience ratings for Catherine McKinnon's songs when I produced her first album, *The Voice of an Angel*. These were the songs that had the highest index. Otherwise, we simply used the audience ratings to keep an eye on how we were doing.

Milt Isnor: Manny had really great people skills. People would do their best for Manny. It wasn't a screech and holler kind of thing with myself or performers. He was back there with a knowing look, or a smile. He got the best out of people. Plus, he surrounded himself with good people. He had a good knack of finding talent and appreciating it, also delegating authority — not a lot of people are good at that.

Lorne White: Manny was always very unassuming, but you always knew where the power was. He is a terrific leader. No one was ever offended. He showed his appreciation to every one of us, recognizing that each one of us was making a contribution. He always let you know that he appreciated what you were doing.

❖

Everyone has their own Fred McKenna story. Fred was a musical genius. His ear for all kinds of music is legendary, and his sense of rhythm was uncanny. At the same time, Fred McKenna inspired everyone to hear country music in a fresh way.

A favourite of people familiar with Singalong *is Fred McKenna, the fellow usually sitting down, always with his guitar flat on his lap. "I play 11 instruments and the only ones I haven't turned upside down yet are the piano and bass fiddle." A bear of a man, he looks a lot older than his 37 years. When he sings he makes you feel so good. He grins a lot and his lips seem to get caught in those large uneven teeth so that it looks like he's singing out of the corners of his mouth.*

— *Weekend Magazine*

❖

Edith Butler, Lorne White, Karen Oxley and Hal Kemspter (sitting) on the set of Singalong Jubilee *(1968).*

REMEMBERING SINGALONG JUBILEE

Hal Kempster: *Singalong* may not have become what it did without Fred, because of his influence on it in the early years. He was the catalyst around which our music was built, and on which everybody built afterwards.

Elan Stuart: I had arrived there with no expertise at playing guitar or anything else, and I needed a guitarist. So, Manny collected a few local musicians, and they came in and played. We decided on a very simple song called *Go Away From My Window*. Manny and I listened to the guitarists, and then Freddie came in and there was an immediate empathy, I mean, I just loved him. And he played so perfectly. He just felt the chords. And, I just looked at Manny and I said "This guy's got to be the guitarist. He's wonderful."

Above: Elan Stuart and Bud Spencer.
Inset: Elan Stuart.

From then on, it was just an absolute delight. He and his wife Melva were absolutely wonderful people, and we had a lot of good afternoons rehearsing songs, drinking Schooner beer, and chatting about the old times, singing all the songs. It was great. He was a wonderful, wonderful musician. A very sensitive human being.

Bill Langstroth: Where do you begin talking about Fred McKenna? Fred was musically able to accompany any soloist that turned up. He could make an arrangement of that accompaniment so that if anybody wanted to join in, or if anybody should be brought in the chorus, or

Fred McKenna (1968).

THE SHOW'S FOUNDATIONS

anything else, it all fit. His musicality went deeper than we know. I don't think I ever appreciated him fully. I loved him dearly and had him as a guest on the *Messer* show. With his guitar played in that strange lap position, he could bring so much music out of those six strings. A voice that was lower-ranged, he was a country singer way ahead of his time in many ways. A wonderful inspiration to us!

Marg Ashcroft: He was always so much aware of everything that was going on, in spite of his blindness. He was an incredible man, incredible human being, and a very good friend. And I look back sometimes and think how fortunate I was to have known Fred for the time that I did.

Milt Isnor: When you make a list of the people you are

Fred McKenna.

much better off for having known, Fred McKenna is number one or two on that list of mine. Musically, he could play anything, and he played in an unorthodox fashion. He played the fiddle upside down, he played the guitar on his lap, and he played the mandolin vertically. He was blind, he didn't know the proper way to hold anything. He should have been famous, because he could do anything.

Dave McClafferty: Someone working on one of the *Singalong* shows had a toy stringed instrument that they had gotten for their kids. It looked like a ukulele but no one could get it to tune as a uke. They tried other tunings, but it just didn't seem right. They handed it to Freddie McKenna, and Fred tuned it and played it with no problem. Someone asked, "Well Fred, is it a uke or what?" Freddie answered, "I don't know, I just tuned it till I liked the sound and played it."

Ken Tobias: What I remember most about Fred is that he was a great musician — not a good musician, but a great musician. He played violin, mandolin, slap guitar, the best slap guitar player you ever heard.

Marg Ashcroft.

REMEMBERING SINGALONG JUBILEE

Jack Lilly: For me, being the drummer, Fred McKenna had excellent timing. If it was off time, he could tell you, and he had the best ears in the world. If there was one string off key a mile away, he could tell you which one it was. He was just amazing to play with. I used to go to Fred's motel room — Karen and I — and I would play with my

Jack Lilly.

brushes on one of his chairs. He thought that I had excellent timing, so we got along very well because, as far as I was concerned, if you just listened to Fred, you would know where the timing was.

Gene MacLellan: When I think of Fred, I think of a guitar player. He and I came from the same school, only he graduated.

Chalmers Doane: Freddie had great ears, and his background was basically country but it didn't matter. The guy had ears and could play anything. You didn't have to play it twice for Freddie! We had to put up with a lot of nonsense at times, but in my book, for Freddie it was worth it. When you get somebody with that kind of exceptional genius, it is worth it for me.

Davey Wells: When I joined *Singalong Jubilee*, it was a great honour for me to meet someone like Fred McKenna, who taught me another aspect of music that I hadn't known: the country side of things.

Garth Proude: Coming from rock 'n' roll, and moving to Halifax and getting into rhythm and blues and jazz and so on, country just wasn't a cool thing to appreciate. He showed me what can be really done with country music.

Davey Wells.

THE SHOW'S FOUNDATIONS

across that great conclusion, but it did work for us. If a performer reached Fred, then that performer was in. If the performer didn't reach Fred, then perhaps we would never book them again, or we would look to change their act somehow. This was an unofficial status that he had. Fred McKenna was the country heart of *Singalong Jubilee*.

❖

Many who knew Karen Oxley believe that her musical talent should have earned her greater fame and fortune, but timing and fashion were unkind to her. Karen clearly had a musical maturity way beyond her years. She was not out of her twenties when she became musical director of *Singalong Jubilee* nor when the series ended in 1974.

Above: Anne Murray perfoms solo on an early Singalong *broadcast.*

The Dropouts, Christmas (1968).

Anne Murray: Freddie introduced me to country music. Up until that time, I had really ignored it, and I was sort of thrown into the centre of choruses, singing behind Freddie, and I got very much caught up in it. And so, as I say, I was never much interested before then, and before I knew it I was a fan, because of Freddie. Eventually, when I won my Juno one year, I gave the Juno to Freddie, 'cos I won it for country music, and so I thought he should have it.

Manny Pittson: As years went by, Fred became more of a guru to the kids on the show. If we reached Fred with a performance, we knew that we didn't have to worry about audience appreciation indexes, we had somehow reached the mood of our audience. I don't know how we came

❖

Chalmers Doane: Karen was an exceptional singer. There are very few people in the whole country that could sing like Karen; very, very few. I never heard her sing a note out of tune. I had her as a student, and she performed and recorded with Lorne and me, and she was exceptional. She wasn't a strong instrumentalist. I spent quite a number of years trying to teach her different instruments, and she never gave up. She played ukulele and tuba, and worked like heck at it. But she was a natural singer, and had the feel for timing and all those other things in an amazing way.

Milt Isnor: Karen Oxley was, to my mind, the heart of *Singalong Jubilee*. She was the musical leader of the chorus. She had a great sense of humour. When something would strike her funny — someone would fart or something — she would laugh for 20 minutes. She was a real sweetheart, everyone loved her.

Bob Theakston: There were those who were real pros that you could always depend on. Karen was a real pro. She always had her songs down. When Karen was the chorus leader, she whipped them into shape.

Clary Croft: Karen Oxley was the backbone of the show. You heard Karen sing *Poor Little Girls of Ontar-i-o,* but then at a party, when you heard her sing jazz and blues, you thought there has to be an audience for this as well. She was magnificent.

Georges Hébert: She was a really, really good singer, and technically speaking, she was one of the best around. She was really great with us. We backed her up a lot in clubs, too. She had a little bit more swing. She could go jazzy, she wasn't country or anything, she was more pop. She was fabulous.

Garth Proude: In those days, they were looking for a young beauty kind of thing. Karen was a fine looking girl, but not the look that

Brian Ahern (1961).

the record companies wanted in those days. Everyone looked up to her as a great musician. Karen was the one that should have done better.

Karen Oxley: I was never terrifically happy out front as a soloist on television. But I love doing radio, because then all that counts is what you do with your throat, and how you phrase a line, how you sing a note, which is what I do best.

Lorne White: I always considered Karen to be the most musical of all of us. She was extremely talented, had a terrific voice, a tremendous knowledge of harmonies. Whenever we were rehearsing as the Dropouts both Vern and I benefited from her expertise. I always felt that had Karen been more glamorous, there was no one any lovelier than Karen in her personality. She was a great lady. But her appearance was not starlike enough. Her musical talent was so great that today she would have been able to go on and become very famous. But back then, there were certain qualities that were anticipated in performing artists, in 'stars.' She had leadership qualities that were tremendous. As musical director, she was a real asset to the show. She was a tremendous loss when she passed away.

❖

Brian Ahern only performed with the show for three summer seasons from 1964 to 1966, but his impact extended far beyond those years. His musical genius was quickly recognized, and he became musical director for both *Singalong* and *Frank's Bandstand*. There was a lot of musical cross-fertilization between

Cast and guests on 'old mill' set.

the two shows and their differing folk/hootenanny and rock 'n' roll styles. He brought Ken Tobias, Steve Rhymer, Garth Proude, and Jack Lilly to *Singalong*, and helped develop and improve the CBC's 'Halifax sound.'

He eventually became one of the most successful music producers in North America in the past 40 years.

❖

Brian Ahern: I came in with Donny Burke, as a member of his folk group. I somehow infiltrated the cast of *Singalong Jubilee*. I couldn't read music, and most of the others couldn't either. So there was no other way to do it but to imagine it in your head and then sing it to them. I'd listen to the song, and if it was too long I'd have them cut it. If it was boring, I'd design some instrumental passage, and I'd sketch out a chord chart for the musicians and pass it out, and just glare at them until they got it right.

Ken Tobias: Without Brian there would have been no *Singalong*. He is as important as Manny, as far as I am concerned. Brian is a genius. We were doing a Christmas show in the summer time. It was very warm. Nobody felt like working, everyone was in shorts. Brian was leaning back in a chair sound asleep. Karen was trying to work out the background vocals, the harmonies for the sopranos.

Someone went over to him, "Brain, Brain," that's what we called him. He wakes up and somebody says we are working on this vocal part, and he says, "What's the song?" Everybody starts laughing, and they explain what the song is. "And, you are working on the background vocals?"

He sits there for a couple of minutes, and starts to play

The Don Burke Four: (left to right) Don Burke, guitar; Brian Ahern, guitar; Kay Porter, singer; and Marilyn Davies, singer.

the tune from top to bottom in jerky sections. Then he says, "Okay, tenors sing this, altos sing this, sopranos sing this, let's go." When they did, it was like heaven. Nobody was getting it, and everybody at the same time got the same feeling — this guy is amazing.

Brian had the first electric twelve-string guitar in Canada. He was way ahead of anyone. He was the first guy to do sound on sound in Halifax. Brian was doing sound layering on those two-track machines, like the Beatles. This was a guitar player extraordinaire. He taught me how to play acoustic guitar using a pick and still be able to finger pick. He had patience up the whazoo, more patience than anyone else did. I can't say enough about him.

Manny Pittson: Brian Ahern is a very central, very important figure to the show. He had an instinct for sound, and instinct for what to do next when you arranged a song and when you recorded it. Don't forget, Brian learned everything on the job at CBC Halifax. I opened the studio for him and said, "Go for it." He came out with some very commercial stuff when he wanted to, and some weird experimental stuff when he wanted to. He was the musical axle, the fulcrum, for both *Frank's Bandstand* and *Singalong Jubilee* for a number of years. A more important person didn't exist for the show.

Wayne Grigsby: Who is going to produce the sound? Well, here's this punk kid Ahern, he seems to have some ideas.

THE SHOW'S FOUNDATIONS

They were doing stuff that was way more sophisticated than their technology allowed. Brian was stealing pages out of the Phil Spector Wall of Sound approach. They found a way to make it interesting.

Brian Ahern: With *Singalong Jubilee*, people like Hal Kempster and Marg Ashcroft would come in and really enjoy themselves, and it made me realize that having a career in music was something to be cherished. If they would come in and work after they did their day job, they must have really loved it. So I started thinking, "Maybe this is something I should consider."

❖

Gene MacLellan's song writing for *Singalong Jubilee* may well be the show's most enduring legacy. Virtually every one of his songs was first heard on *Singalong*. And, of course, it was through *Singalong* that his partnership with Anne Murray was forged and the biggest Canadian hit of all time was born. *Snowbird* has now been recorded by more than 100 different artists — more than any other Canadian song.

❖

Bill Langstroth: Gene MacLellan came to us through the *Messer* show. Gene was a voice on tape that Don Messer had in his box of people who wanted to get on the show. I was not sure that the voice was what we wanted, to tell you the truth. I was not that keen on the voice, but the song was *The Call* and the other song he proposed doing was *Snowbird*, and both those songs appeared in their initial forms on the *Messer* show.

Anne Murray: Gene MacLellan was a very unique talent. He sang with such ease. I loved the way he sang, just a natural singer, very soulful. Just oozed music. Our voices were very compatible.

Georges Hébert: He was a huge, huge influence on everybody. His songwriting and his songs, you just wanted to play those songs and back him up in everything.

(Right to Left) Jackie Harris, Gene MacLellan and Garth Proude perform live.

Clary Croft: Gene's ratings were never particularly high on the show, but Manny knew that he had an artist of such incredible calibre here, that he was willing to say we are going to continue pushing this. Now we all know Gene as one of Canada's finest songwriters.

Manny Pittson: We ignored the ratings with regard to Gene MacLellan. I think the audience found him a little harsh, a little 'unsweet' for *Singalong Jubilee*. He used to make in the low 60s, whereas McKinnon and Murray were in the high 70s or low 80s, with the show always being in the 75 to 79 range. With Gene, we felt it was better just to swallow the bitter pill and have him around as resident songwriter, and take the risk that we weren't going to sink our ship by having him do that.

Milt Isnor: When Gene was writing *Hand In the Hand*, we didn't have a title for it. We would be sitting around chatting and Gene would be writing. We called it 'Gene's God Song.' That's what we called it when we first recorded it.

Anne Murray and Gene MacLellan perform a duet for Singalong's *tenth anniversary broadcast.*

Bill Langstroth: It did not take much of a stretch to put the new kid on the block — that would be Anne Murray — together with Gene MacLellan. When Anne heard the song, she thought, "That's for me, that's the kind of stuff I want to do." It was poetry. That's her background.

Anne Murray: It goes without saying that he was a great songwriter. He was a very clever lyric writer, a lot of his lyrics were brilliant. Gene was doing a guest spot on *Don Messer* and Bill called me and said, "I would like you to meet this guy. He has written some songs, which are very good." So we met during a break in a conference room.

When Gene came up and sang me these songs, I was totally in awe because I had never heard an original song. I had been singing other peoples' songs. I said, "These are really good," and he said, "Would you like them?" I said, "Why, yeah!" Brian and I were talking about doing another album, so what a start. I had *Snowbird* and *Just Biding my Time. Just Biding My Time* he wrote for me. It's one of two songs written for me. It was the one that was supposed to be the hit.

Gene MacLellan: I remember that day. I was really nervous, with her sitting there especially. I did a couple of duets with Anne. Yeah, I really enjoyed it. I was nervous then, too. You're singing with a pretty heavy singer, you know? And I had come from the boonies.

THE SHOW'S FOUNDATIONS

Jack MacAndrew: Gene wrote songs because he had to write songs. There was no other way for Gene. It was truly the way he expressed himself. The genius of Gene MacLellan as a songwriter was the genius of every great artist and that is the capacity to express profound and universal things about the human condition in the simplest of words and phrases — that's genius and in his own way, that's what he was.

❖

Bill Langstroth brought an energy and a 'zaniness' to *Singalong* that was not common to television in the early 1960s. He never took himself too seriously, and if he tried, the family would straighten him out. He was the perfect host for the show, because he never outshone anybody.

❖

Anne Murray: I remember vaguely having seen *Singalong Jubilee* [before her initial audition]. I don't remember much except for Bill Langstroth, who was so outrageous. I remember him, and he stuck in my head because he was a bit of a kook. Bill was the Lewis of Dean Martin and Jerry Lewis, playing off of Jim Bennet, and I remember him, thinking he was silly.

Bill Langstroth in 'Nellie' costume.

Georges Hébert: Bill Langstroth was a real leader. When they did a *Singalong Jubilee* number he was standing on a chair, conducting, so that they can see him. He was definitely a presence to be reckoned with. He was so funny. He made everybody laugh. He is not shy, put it that way. He takes charge, and that is a good thing. In a situation like that, you need someone to take charge.

Clary Croft: Bill was always very jovial. He was the fellow who could get people up. When things got a little bit cloudy on the set, and I don't mean through animosity, I just mean that at three o'clock in the morning, when you were in makeup at 6 p.m., things can get a little bit down, and Bill could bring things back up again. Bill was the clown of the show, and I mean clown in the best sense of the word — the person who talked about the soul of the show but showed it through humour and spontaneity and levity.

Lorne White: Whenever you saw Bill perform in person, he always had his audiences in the palm of his hand. He

Georges Hébert.

was always a gentleman, nobody ever got torn down by anything he did on stage. I always like to think of Bill as another Red Skelton in a sense, because Red Skelton was one of the humourists who never injured anyone, never tore anyone down. That was the kind humour that Bill brought to his audiences.

Bill Langstroth: You may have seen the mobile that we did on Citadel Hill, where the tune that was playing as we cavorted around Citadel Hill. And 'cavorted' covers it, it was a big cavort on a bicycle, falling off, rolling around in drag. It was just about as crazy as you can get. I was a fearless performer. I have no idea where that came from, I just knew that it seemed appropriate at the time.

Bill and Jim clowning around during a remote shoot in (1969).

5

TOO GOOD TO LAST

In the spring of 1970, Bill Langstroth and Anne Murray moved to Toronto, though Anne remained a frequent guest on the show for the next few years. Tom Kelly was brought in from Toronto to host the show for its final three seasons and certainly had a formidable role to fill. Manny Pittson was not re-offered his contract for the 1973-74 season and was ready to move on with his career in broadcasting and in music. Ted Regan was brought in to direct.

Bill Langstroth, Karen Oxley, Manny Pittson, Jim Bennet and Lorne White cut the cake at Singalong's *tenth anniversary celebration.*

time as [Manny Pittson] did. My reasoning for that was that I had worked with him for so long, and I knew that if a new producer came in he was going to change the image of that show. That's a producer's prime concern. You bring a new man in, he can't make it look like the same show it was. Now on some shows that may help, but I felt in *Singalong's* case it would hurt. And boy, they did change the image of the show. I am not going to say for better or worse, but they sure did change it.

❖ ❖

Bill Langstroth: I left the show after the 1970-71 season. Just felt that I had done everything I could. When Manny left it wasn't the same show, and I really wasn't interested in working with the show the way it was being conceived. I did not have a sense that the program was light-hearted any more. We were becoming heavy-handed, and I wasn't interested in being part of that.

Fred McKenna: I decided that I would leave at the same

The show was still enjoying critical acclaim.

Some dismiss Singalong *as just another half-hour of straight, pleasant songs. But they're wrong. Over the years, some of the most talented musical artists in the country have graduated from the show, perhaps more than from any other single Canadian production. The reason is this low-budget show itself professional, fast-moving, non-gimmicky, simple, and sincere and*

73

Cast members performing on Singalong's *10th Anniversary broadcast.*

thoroughly Canada. 'A fresh, wide awake, sunshine show,' someone has called it. While it has a distinctly Maritime flavour, its appeal, obviously, is national. But Singalong's *most outstanding characteristic, perhaps, is that it doesn't imitate. The current style in New York, Los Angeles or Toronto doesn't matter — Halifax has its own.*

— Weekend Magazine

Singalong Jubilee had retained the *Don Messer Jubilee* audience, at least on the CBC stations. Where the show could be seen in the major cities, it had a stronger audience than *Hogan's Heroes* or though less than *Laugh In* or the Saturday night NHL hockey broadcasts. However, in the early 1970s, at least half of the CBC audience saw CBC programming via privately owned affiliated stations, and *Singalong* was not carried on the CBC affiliates.

The private stations were always seeking to carry the more profitable American programming and were constantly renegotiating which of the CBC-originated programming they were required to carry. *Singalong*

TOO GOOD TO LAST

Bill Langstroth performing solo on Singalong's *7th season.*

Jubilee was a casualty of this jockeying.

Then the CBC network began to move *Singalong Jubilee* around on the schedule, but the *Singalong* audience followed the program with exceptional loyalty. In May 1972, Arthur Laird, head of the CBC Audience Research Department, sent a memo to Sandy Lumsden, program director of CBHT, warning the network about the loyalty of the *Singalong* audience. He had been working on a formal report on the *Singalong* audiences over the past three years since it had replaced *Messer*, but the report had been cancelled, perhaps because it did not tell the network what it wanted to hear. But Laird was not prepared to let his work go ignored.

The keynote is consistency. Despite the many changes in cast over this period (most notably the loss of Anne Murray, Bill Langstroth and Gene MacLellan, and the addition of Tom Kelly, Clary Croft and Penny MacAuley), there has been little or no change in the size of the Singalong *audience. This audience stability (825,000–900,000 viewers) even extends over different time slots and seems little affected by variations in opposition programming on the private network…*

Currently in the Wednesday seven-thirty time slot, the Singalong *audience splits like this: children under 12 – 13 percent, teens to age 17 – 9 percent, young adults to 34 – 20 percent, adults 35 – 49 – 14*

REMEMBERING SINGALONG JUBILEE

the show was being killed quite deliberately. They had their reasons to be suspicious of Ted Regan, and certainly were not comfortable with the changes he brought to *Singalong*.

❖

Ted Regan: The CBC wanted to spice up *Singalong* so that was my objective. Because I was from Toronto, I had a little bit more of a national perspective and some chutzpah. I was asked to come down by Sandy Lumsden, program director at CBHT at the time. The concern was that the network might be thinking of taking *Singalong* off because it had been on air for too many years and they wanted to liven it up. It was a mix between *Don Messer* and *Hymn Sing*, which came out of Winnipeg. *Hymn Sing* was just a chorus of 16 people literally standing in robes, and that was it. At the time the *Jubilee Singers* were doing a little bit of movement, but mainly it was singing in a group. So, they wanted to jazz it up with the hope that the network would keep it on. They wanted some fresh blood, which I brought.

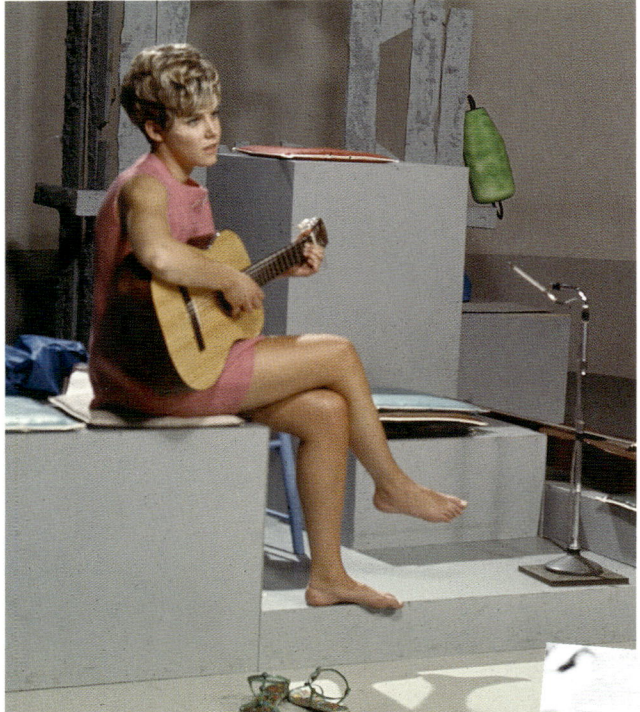

Above: Anne Murray singing barefoot (1967).
Right: Tom Kelly.

A new, contemporary look in style and sound. The half-hour Halifax music series is in for a challenging year, with a wholly new format, pace and tempo in the offing. Set designs will not be locked in, but will be

percent, and over 50 – 44 percent. The age structure of the Singalong *audience is much the same as that of* Tommy Hunter.

Finally, the network moved the show to the Saturday night timeslot after the hockey games. Depending on the length of the game, it might not air at all. The Remembrance Day show prepared in the fall of 1973, one they were all so proud of, never did get to air. This scheduling change also meant that *Singalong* was now aired in the Maritimes at 11:30 p.m., which reduced its local audience considerably.

Cast and crew to this day believe that

76

Shirley Eikhard and Tom Kelly.

representative of any down-by-the-water location in Canada, a friendly meeting place where people can just sing along together.
— *CBC Press Release*

Clary Croft: Tom Kelly probably had the hardest job on *Singalong* of anybody. He came into something so well established, also something, in my opinion, that was starting to be crucified by the corporation. Some of us in the *Singalong* family refer to it as they started to make the show 'right-Toronto.' Tom was a lovely man, good songwriter, nice singer, and good guitar player. Very personable. That tall lanky loping kind of guy that they literally had to put a piece of foam rubber underneath his foot so that it would not be picked up when he was singing and banging on the

microphone. But, he was coming in to front a show that I think was on its way out.

Tom Kelly: I was co-host for the last three years, and I think maybe that the show had reached its high point before it was actually off the air. I think that it was starting to fade.

Then in the last year of the show, a new executive producer was brought in from Toronto and brought out the big broom. He completely changed the look of the show. Everybody was kind of aghast. It was a theatrical showbiz approach that we had not had up to that point. They used to call *Singalong Jubilee*, '*Hymn Sing* with a beat.' It was just good music well done, that was what it was.

Milt Isnor: In the last years, it was bad. Anne and Bill had left. Manny stayed on and brought Tom Kelly in – that wasn't too bad. Tom was good. Tom was a likeable fellow. Manny had some of his more creative moments. The cast changed quite a bit. Then they brought in a new director. He tried some slick production things. He tried multifaceted lenses, which were then available. More

Cast at Christmas.

production value and no soul. I think the show was based on its heart and soul. He made it too 'Toronto'. They tend to overproduce.

Garth Proude: The show really changed drastically in those last couple of years. It was a new producer. It wasn't Manny Pittson any more. He wanted to put on the *Tommy Hunter* type of look. He was trying to get people to move around, a little bit of dancing. It was a completely different format, rather than a 'singalong jubilee' with everyone sitting around a campfire singing. It was show time. It kind of ruined the show. By the end of it, we were just going in and doing a job, rather than a family getting together like it used to be.

Ted Regan: To try and liven things up, and to be sensible about choreographing people and movements, to ensure that the way people moved on camera would look natural, I brought in a choreographer from the National Ballet, Anne Ditchburn. Anne came down for two or three rehearsals over a month, and she was showing people how to do body movements, how to walk and talk.

This might sound a little bit silly but performing on camera really involves some performance. It took a little choreography, nothing very detailed, nothing very difficult, which turned out to be a good idea. I was trying to make them look better on camera. There are a lot of ways you can walk across camera, different ways you can carry your body. Everybody has their own body language, even in sitting and relaxing. But it wasn't fun. God bless her, she really tried hard to get them to like her and respect her.

It was a bit of a giggle to everybody to think that we were going to bring in a choreographer to teach them to walk. "I have been walking all my life, what's the big deal?" She did teach them some good things, but it may have a little bit overkill on my part. It did not go over very well.

Wayne Grigsby: The plans he had for the show seemed totally bizarre to me. I had one meeting with Ted and what he was talking about made no sense to me, and I said so and so my contract was not renewed. With what

Catherine MacKinnon.

they were going to do to the show I said, "Why don't you just kill it? It is not going to fix it."

Karen (Oxley) would call me in the last season and would tell me these stories and we would just laugh. The whole idea of Anne Ditchburn trying to get Fred McKenna and Howie Solverson to do little dance steps was beyond belief. This was so much Toronto. It was bizarre. They are singers and pickers. You want some comedy routines? Wrong show!

Catherine McKinnon: From the time they brought the Toronto crew in, they said they were going to make the show relevant. It was the beginning of the end. I remember Anne Ditchburn not knowing anything about a song called *Peter Emberly*. You have to sing together as a trio, that's what you do. That's what the music dictates.

She had the boys in different places. There was Karen dancing with a broom.

When I came on the show, they had this two pages of dialogue they wanted me and Trish to do. I said it's demeaning, and I won't do this. This show wasn't about dialogue, it was about the celebration of music, that was what people tuned in for. It didn't take long for us to be cancelled because they took away the essence of what it was. It was a show about music and the joy, and we had joy singing it, and that went through that lens and people loved that.

Marg Ashcroft: All the things we had done before, our spontaneity seemed to be lost in the shuffle. The show was popular because it was just like a group of people sitting down around a campfire, or on a bunch of rocks. We used to have a hard time keeping nylons because they used to rip our nylons, these artificial rocks. When Ted came, he wanted us to be a little more uptown Toronto, maybe, and we would do blocking. We didn't feel as comfortable. I guess most of us would feel that way.

Ryan's Fancy were guests on the show and they were singing an Irish song about a guy waiting for his hanging. Anne Ditchburn, the choreographer, wanted more reaction from us. She was trying to direct those of us who were on camera and could be seen during the taping of this mournful song that *Ryan's Fancy* was singing. She was trying to get us to be more animated, if you will, and trying to get us to smile or whatever.

One of them said to her, "My god, woman, how can they be happy? The man's going to his hanging," and totally blew the whole place apart. Everyone was on the floor laughing. It was one of the great stories from *Singalong*.

Tom Kelly.

Tom Kelly: We laughed and laughed and laughed. That was the breaking point. There was the vision that this was never going to fly, but for whatever reason it was imposed on the show. It just didn't work, like trying to put a strange suit on somebody, but it wasn't immediately obvious. It came at us from a number of different points, from a number of different people.

Ted Regan: Scheduling *Singalong Jubilee* after the hockey game on Saturday nights was also very dangerous because we never knew how long the program was going to be. Saturday night was a great time, and we were glad to get that, but we were not very happy with the ten-thirty time slot because of the uncertainty of the game ending. I think that I managed to negotiate that if we had less than 10 minutes, they would not put the program on at all.

However, with the program that we shot for Remembrance Day, shot down on board the ships, with the singers gathered around all the military equipment, that did not get on because of the hockey game, which was a terrible thing because it was a gorgeous show. I don't think that an audience has ever seen this show. I remember it being a horrible disappointment.

The network had a way of moving programs to terrible time slots for things they were going to trash. I would have put *Singalong* on before the hockey game. That would have been an excellent time slot.

Clary Croft: The show was widely successful in the late sixties, early seventies. I frankly don't know why it was chosen to be slaughtered, but I firmly believe that it did not die of its own accord. We have seen it happen in the Maritimes before. When we do something successful down here, it is either taken to Upper Canada to be 'improved,' or else they bring the 'improvers' down. And that is what

(From right to left) Tom Kelly, Karen Oxley, Sandy Hurford and Clarke Brown pose for a publicity shot, Remembrance Day 1973.

happened with *Singalong*. They brought Toronto writers down.

Then, they put the show on to be broadcast after the hockey game. Your demographics show you that most of your audience is well over 50, many of them are between 60 and 80. Who stays up to eleven-thirty, twelve, unless you are a hockey fan? And then you may be pre-empted and may only get the last 10 minutes of *Singalong*. It is the kiss of death.

Lorne White: We anticipated the dying of the show, figuring there was an edict out of Toronto that said that it was time for this to stop, in spite of the appeal that the show had across the country. That's what we were thinking at the time, and how unjust it was. We had the feeling that they sent a producer down here to say, "This show is not going anywhere." The old way was working as far as the public was concerned. The mail was fantastic. To think that people took the time to write and say that they loved the show.

❖

Audience ratings in broadcasting are difficult to assess at the best of times because they can be used to bolster whatever conclusion is desired. In that final season, it is clear that whatever audience it had — or didn't have — *Singalong Jubilee* was not going to survive. The heart and soul had left *Singalong* and the audience knew it. The magic was gone. There was no protest anywhere when *Singalong Jubilee* was cancelled. It had a good long run, but it was time to move on.

Clary Croft.

❖

Ted Regan: The network said at the beginning of the season that they were looking at possibly cancelling the series, and the audience rating at the time was 6.0 audience share. I made an arrangement with the head of Variety at the time that if I got the audience rating up to 10 by Christmas that they would leave it on the air. The ratings that came in January showed that our audience rating was 11.6, so we had more than achieved our goal. I sent a one page memo to the head of Variety in Toronto and put a huge 11.6 and signed my name, Ted.

I was then asked to come down to Toronto for a meeting some time in February, which I assumed was going to be about arrangements to continue the concept. I was taken out to dinner, and halfway through the salad, they told me that regardless of the ratings they were going to drop *Singalong* and put another program in.

That was how I got the news, and so I had to tell the singers and the Jubilee gang back in Halifax, and that was not a good taste. I was the new boy coming to town, and here I was coming in with the bad news. It did not feel very good, and I didn't enjoy that very much.

Georges Hébert: I still hold a few resentments at the way it was done. The show was going along just fine, and I don't think that it was running out of steam. This is my take on it. They had made such a mistake canning *Don Messer* and they had such flack about it, and they wanted to can *Singalong*. They wanted to can it, but they didn't know how to do it in such a way that it wouldn't offend people. So they brought a producer down from Toronto, they let Manny go.

REMEMBERING SINGALONG JUBILEE

Bill Langstroth leads the cast in song.

Wayne Grigsby: It wasn't dissimilar to what happened to *Messer*, that people sitting in Toronto got embarrassed by *Singalong*. It was kind of 'hickish', or 'hayseed', or something. The folk thing had passed and it couldn't be hip in Toronto terms. So they made the moves that were necessary to do that. They were just wrong, and it's not the first time the network's been wrong about shows that they feel awkward about. There's a long and rich tradition of the network getting it wrong. This was another one.

Bill Langstroth: I would hear people afterwards say, "Oh, we miss your show." Of course they did, because it was a habit. Was it a good habit? Were we really telling you anything new? Were we purely entertainment? I don't know? I felt we were moving on. I think that's the way Mr. Messer felt, to tell you the truth.

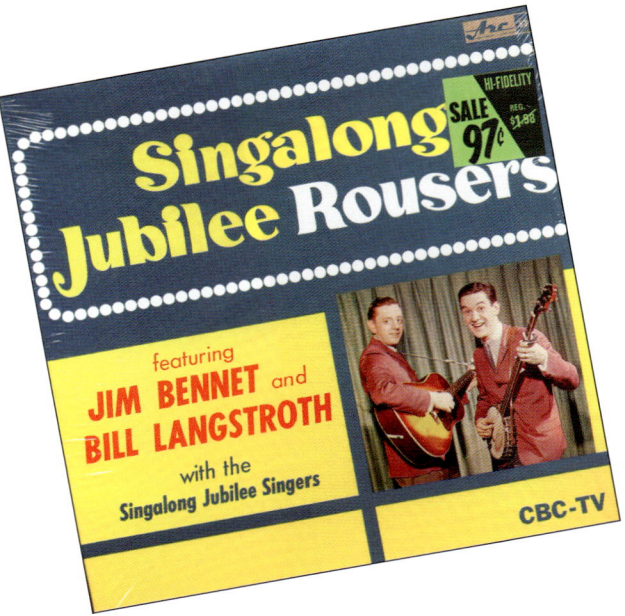

TOO GOOD TO LAST

Cast members singing together on location.
Right: Cover of Anne Murray's first album.

❖

Don Messer's Jubilee may have been watched by more people. Helen Creighton and Clary Croft, as collectors of folk songs, undoubtedly collected and preserved more Maritime music. Television specials over the years, featuring Anne Murray, Rita MacNeil, Natalie MacMaster, Men of the Deeps, Great Big Sea, and dozens of others have clearly sold more LPs and CDs than *Singalong Jubilee* ever did.

But none can yet claim to giving voice to the range of new performers and new music with the same vitality and authenticity, and with the same success, over such an extended period. *Singalong Jubilee* had an uncanny knack for giving a national stage to the performers and music of Atlantic Canada and prepared the way for Stan Rogers, Ashley MacIsaac, the Rankins, J. P. Cormier, Crush, and even Gary Beals, to mention only a few. The annual *East Coast Music Awards* shows these days, continue the showcasing of talent that *Singalong Jubilee* began.

❖

Wayne Grigsby: I was staggered by how good the band was and how rich the history of the show was. I loved the

83

REMEMBERING SINGALONG JUBILEE

way the entire crew worked, and the musicians. I had worked with musicians in Montreal, but they were never as good as the people here. For me, they were the top of the heap, they were the class act. It wasn't in Toronto or Vancouver. The only show that rivalled it for me was the *Guess Who* version of *Music Hop*. I thought there was great work being done here and most of the people on the show didn't realize how great it was.

Singalong gave more to me than I gave to the show. It made me realize that you don't have to be in the major metropolis to be doing good work. In fact, sometimes to be at a distance means that you get to do better work because you are not constantly being supervised or trying to do the trendy thing. There is great talent everywhere in the country, and you can be wherever you want to be to do good work.

Manny Pittson: *Singalong* (like *Messer* before it) became a Canadian original — a show that dared to be different in style, presentation and content. We're not likely to witness this phenomenon again.

The Singalong *cast (1974) (from right to left): Patrician Anne McKinnon, Tom Kelly, Karen Oxley, Hal Kempster, Michael Scott, [unidentified], Clarke Brown, Nancy deLong, Jack Lilly, Marg Ashcroft, Sandy Hurford and Lorne White.*

6

PROFILES AND CREDITS

Brian Ahern grew up in Halifax and began forming his own music groups in the early 1960s. Brian joined *Singalong* in 1964 as a guitarist and member of The Don Burke Four, becoming musical director for *Singalong* as well as *Frank's Bandstand*. Brian moved to Toronto in 1966 to work with ARC Records where he produced LPs for many of the *Singalong* alumni, most notably Anne Murray. He then moved to Los Angeles and eventually Nashville as a record producer working with Emmylou Harris, Johnny Cash and many others.

Audrey Alexander grew up in Halifax, beginning a performing career at the age of 10 with *Don Messer's Jubilee*. She joined *Singalong Jubilee* in the mid-sixties for two seasons. She sang in the chorus, with duets and trios, and had the occasional solo with *Singalong* while still in high school. She also sang with The Secrets and did further radio and television work. Audrey went on to an extensive recording, directing and teaching career. These days, she is busy performing throughout Atlantic Canada with Alex Vaughan, as Audrey and Alex, and winning multiple ECMA awards.

Tom Anthes joined the CBC in Halifax as a set designer in 1967. His first major assignment was the sets for *Singalong* in the summer of 1968, a task he continued for the duration of the series. He is also an accomplished artist. Tom continues to design sets at CBC Halifax.

Marg Ashcroft is originally from Stewiacke, Nova Scotia, and moved to Halifax to train as a nurse. She was singing with the Nova Scotia Girl Singers when she auditioned and became a chorus member with *Singalong* for the 1963 and 1964 seasons and from 1966 to 1974. She was dubbed 'Mog' by the wardrobe lady. After *Singalong,* Marg sang choral backup on television for a number of years. She then joined the Aeolian Singers and the Chebucto Singers. Marg currently lives in Hammonds Plains, Nova Scotia.

Paul Baylis is from Toronto and joined the CBC in 1953 as a radio and television announcer. He came to CBC Halifax in 1956 as a production assistant and became a director in 1959. He directed *Don Messer's Jubilee* in the early sixties while Bill Langstroth was busy with *Singalong Jubilee,* then directed *Singalong* for the summers of 1967 and 1968, while Manny Pittson was in Toronto. Over the years, Paul directed every type of program for the CBC in Halifax, except drama. He retired in 1988 and now lives in Charlottetown, PEI.

Jim Bennet began his vocal training in the choir of All Saints Cathedral in Halifax. He joined the CBC in Halifax in the early 1950s and had a 31-year career with CBC radio and television, writing, narrating, announcing and hosting a great variety of programs. He was co-host, soloist, songwriter, versifier, and all-around wit with *Singalong* from its beginning through to 1973. Jim took early retirement in 1981 and joined the family company, Bennet Communications. He has published two books of verse and is now fully retired.

85

REMEMBERING SINGALONG JUBILEE

Don Burke is a Haligonian who began a musical career as a 'folkie' in the early 1960s. He played banjo and guitar with The Townsmen, who performed on *Singalong* for the 1963 season and then disbanded. In 1965, he formed the Don Burke Four and also sang on *Singalong*. Don then traveled to France and formed a French folk trio, Les Troubadours, which performed for the next 20 years. Since 1984, Don remains active with songwriting and the occasional performance, back in Halifax.

Edith Butler is from Paquetville, New Brunswick. She sang in coffee houses as a university student at the University of Moncton in the early 1960s, and appeared on *Singalong* for the 1966 Christmas Day special. Edith became a frequent guest performer, combining Acadian traditional music with her own compositions. She has since travelled and performed around the world to great acclaim. She moved to Montreal in the 1970s and has recorded many albums over the years, developing a strong following in France where she has won numerous awards.

John Allan Cameron was born in Mabou, Cape Breton, and has been performing in public since the age of 13. He joined the *Singalong* crew for the summers of 1967 and 1968, bringing his 'celtic' sound to a national audience. Over the years, he has performed with *Singalong* alumni Anne Murray, Edith Butler, Catherine McKinnon and Robbie MacNeill. John Allan's albums now number 10. He lives in Pickering, Ontario, and was recently awarded the Order of Canada.

David Carr joined the CBC in Halifax in 1956, becoming a film cameraman. He was the director of photography on the *Singalong* outside colour mobiles. David ended his CBC career in the Visual Resources Library, retiring in 1996. He now manages a wine and beer-making supply shop in the North End of Halifax.

Blake Connor joined the CBC in 1954 and worked as a cameraman for his whole career. He was cameraman for virtually all of the *Singalong Jubilee* tapings in Studio One from 1961 to 1974. Blake retired in 1991 and now lives in Centreville, Nova Scotia.

Clary Croft has always been involved with music, growing up in Halifax and Sherbrooke. In 1968, he became a founding member of a folk singing group, The Privateers. He joined *Singalong* in the fall of 1970, dubbed 'little eeck', and was on the show for three seasons: with the chorus, with the house band, and singing solos and duets. Clary has continued performing as well as becoming a folklorist and researcher into traditional Maritime music. As a regular folklore contributor on CBC radio in Nova Scotia, he has now published books on Nova Scotian folklore.

Marilyn Davies-MacDonald is a New Waterford girl, who studied voice at the Maritime Conservatory of Music in Halifax in the early 1960s. She joined the *Singalong* chorus for the 1964-66 summer seasons and also sang with the *Don Burke Four*. She then began a career in journalism, including on-air work with CBC radio and television, and editing *Atlantic Insight*. Marilyn was Director of Public Relations at Dalhousie University until 1996 and now works as a communications consultant.

Graham Day is a Haligonian who was studying law at Dalhousie in the early fifties when he met Manny Pittson.

PROFILES AND CREDITS

A few years later, Manny recruited Graham to become part of the original chorus for *Singalong Jubilee*. He sang with the chorus for four seasons, became the original musical director and was part of the barbershop quartet, Jubilee Four. He left *Singalong* to work with Canadian Pacific in Montreal, then became the head of British Shipbuilders, the Rover Group, and British Aerospace. He was knighted in 1989 for services to British industry. Currently chair of Sobeys, he is director of several companies, and lives in Hantsport.

Chalmers Doane is from Truro. He was leading a dance band, The Swingsters, when he joined *Singalong* for its first season. He sang with the chorus for three seasons, with a quartet, and played ukulele and bass on occasions. He was also a music teacher, director of music education for the Halifax School Board to 1983, and director of music for Nova Scotia Teachers College until 1993. He developed a program for kids playing the ukulele across Canada. Chalmers formed the Uke Trio after *Singalong*. He has contributed to dozens of CBC radio and television broadcasts, and since retirement performs as many as nine different instruments with the Chalmers Doane Trio.

Herb Doane was also born in Truro, singing in church choirs from an early age, and with the Choral Society at Mount Allison University. He joined the *Singalong Jubilee* chorus from 1962 to 1965. At the time, he was working for Nova Scotia Power, and eventually worked for the Nova Scotia government. He is now retired in Halifax.

Ron Dodge is a Haligonian. He was singing with the Scotia Male Chorale when he auditioned to join the *Singalong* chorus in 1961. He sang in the chorus for the first three seasons. He worked with the navy and then with Statistics Canada until he retired in 1989. He still lives in Halifax.

Shirley Eikhard was born in Sackville, New Brunswick, to a musical family. She first appeared on *Singalong* singing her own compositions at the age of 14 in 1970. She was a regular guest for the next three years. Anne Murray's version of *It Takes Time* was Shirley's first hit, and over the years her songs have been performed by Chet Atkins, Emmylou Harris, Kim Carnes, Alannah Myles, Rita Coolidge, Fleetwood Mac, Bonnie Raitt, Cher and dozens of others. She performed regularly across Canada until the mid-1980s, and has released seven albums over the years, composed some 300 songs, written scores for plays, and acted on television. Shirley lives in Toronto and continues to write music.

Ted Flynn was a lawyer in Halifax, where he was recruited to sing for the original pilot for *Singalong*. His bass-baritone was heard for the next two seasons on *Singalong Jubilee*. Ted passed away in 2001.

Eva Fogarty is from Windsor, Nova Scotia. She sang in a country bluegrass group, The Fogartys, and on *Don Messer* on occasion in the 1960s. She joined the *Singalong* chorus for the 1969-70 season. Family responsibilities intervened, but she did resume her singing with bluegrass groups, travelling with Vic Mullen's bands. Eva married Milt Isnor, the long-term floor director for *Singalong*. These days, Eva continues to work in the Halifax Regional Municipality School Board office and sings with the Scotian Aires and the Rolling Tones.

Jeanette (Jay) Gallant-Bona joined the folk-singing trios The Silver Change and then The Privateers in high school. She joined the *Singalong* chorus in 1970 for three seasons, also doing occasional solos, duets, and singing with the *Singalong* group *Six-Pack*. She performed for a number of years until marriage and children diverted her career. She now works at the IWK Hospital in Halifax.

Al Greer is from Joggins, Nova Scotia, and joined the Navy in the late forties. He came to the CBC in Halifax in 1954 as a technician. Later he became the technical producer for all the *Singalong* shows from the beginning through to 1972. In 1972, he became production manager at CBHT, eventually moving to CBC Corner Brook, where he became station manager. Al retired in 1987 and now lives in Truro.

Wayne Grigsby grew up in Montreal and was working on the CBC Montreal TV show *Let's Go* in the late sixties with Manny Pittson. Wayne was then invited to work on *Singalong* as writer, program organizer, and right-hand man to Manny Pittson for the 1971 and 1972 seasons. After *Singalong*, Wayne returned to Montreal hosting CBC radio programming, becoming the arts and entertainment reporter for CBC television, and writing for *MacLean's*. In the 1980s, he turned his hand to writing drama for film and television, such as the CTV series *ENG*, then created and produced the CBC television series *North of 60*. In 1996, he created the dramatic series *Black Harbour* set on the South Shore of Nova Scotia. In 1999, he co-founded the independent film and television production company, Big Motion Pictures in Chester, which produced *Blessed Stranger: After Flight 111* and *Trudeau*.

Georges Hébert is from Moncton, originally playing guitar with the Bunkhouse Boys in the early 1960s, then moving into rock 'n' roll with Roger and the Playboys. This brought him to Halifax and appearances on *Frank's Bandstand*, eventually leading to the *Singalong* house band Musical Friends from 1969 to 1974, where he was dubbed 'Agostini' or 'Jess'. He then played with a variety of groups, including Ian Tyson's Great Speckled Bird, until 1979 when he joined Anne Murray, who he has accompanied for the past 24 years. Georges lives in Bedford, Nova Scotia, performing and operating his own sound studio.

Milt Isnor began work as a lighting technician with CBC television in Halifax in 1956, becoming a floor director for musical programs *Don Messer's Jubilee* and *Singalong Jubilee* in the 1960s. Milt married chorus member Eva Fogarty. Dubbed 'Milton Schmilton, the All-American Canadian' by Bill Langstroth, Milt retired from the CBC in 1995. He currently lives in Dartmouth and winters in Florida.

Tom Kelly is from Thunder Bay, Ontario. A high school teacher in the late 1960s, with aspirations to become a folk singer, he first appeared as a guest soloist on *Singalong Jubilee* in 1970 and then became the co-host in 1971 until the end of the series. Tom returned to the classroom part-time but always continued songwriting. After *Singalong*, Tom also performed in a number of trios with Gene MacLellan but has not performed since the 1980s. These days, he is working on producing a CD of his songs.

Hal Kempster began his lifelong love of music as a choir boy in England, coming to Halifax in 1957 at the age of 27. He joined the chorus of *Singalong Jubilee* in 1963 and remained there for the next 11 years. He worked in the banking industry throughout his career and passed away in July 2002.

Bud Kimball was one of the original singers on the pilot for *Singalong* and sang with the chorus for its first four seasons. He was also part of the quartet Jubilee Four singing barbershop-style close harmonies in the 1963 season. He left *Singalong Jubilee* in 1964 to pursue his law practice in Windsor, and in 1967 was appointed to the Provincial Court of Nova Scotia. He is retired and living on the South Shore of Nova Scotia.

Bill Langstroth is from Hampton, New Brunswick. He attended Mount Allison University in the early 1950s where he established a reputation for performing. He joined CBC Halifax in 1954, almost immediately becoming a TV producer. He produced the *Don Messer Jubilee* throughout its run and the initial pilot for *Singalong Jubilee*, then became the show's host. Bill, also

PROFILES AND CREDITS

known as 'eeck', was the co-host and chorus leader for *Singalong* until 1970, when he moved to Toronto with Anne Murray. Bill and Anne married in 1975, and Bill worked from home on a great variety of film and television projects until 1998. Bill hosted and co-produced with Manny Pittson, the retrospective series *Jubilee Years*. Bill is currently living in Malagash, Nova Scotia.

Jack Lilly is a Haligonian. He was the drummer with Brian Ahern and The Off-Beats on *Frank's Bandstand* from 1964 to 1968. Then he joined *Singalong* from 1969 to 1973 as the drummer for the house band, *Musical Friends*. Jack gave most of the *Singalong* family their nicknames and was himself known as 'Rose'. He married Karen Oxley in 1966. After his *Singalong* days, he played with The Great Speckled Bird for a couple of years and developed music stores in Antigonish and New Glasgow. In recent years, he has played with Frank McKay and the Lincolns' reunions and plays with a local trio, Lowe and Lilly. Jack also owns and operates the Victorian Inn in Antigonish.

Penny Longley came from Toronto for a job at CBC Television in Halifax in 1963. She worked as script assistant for many variety and entertainment programs, including *Singalong Jubilee* from 1964 to 1972. She then left the CBC for five years to focus on her family, returning in 1978. She moved into management in Halifax in the 1990s, and is currently responsible for television programming for the CBC in the Maritimes.

Sharon Martin is from Halifax and sang with the Armdale Chorus. She joined the *Singalong* chorus in her late teens for the 1966 and 1967 seasons. She studied music and theatre at Bishop's University and in Montreal and has sung in musicals all her life, with the Bethany Chorale and as a church soloist. She returned to Nova Scotia in 1975 and worked for many years with the Department of Tourism.

Paul Mason is from Dartmouth. He was playing with the local groups Four Winds and New Directions when he was recruited by Garth Proude in 1970 to play piano for the pre-taping audio recordings on *Singalong Jubilee*. Eventually he played on air and also did vocal arrangements and chord charts until the series ended in 1974. He became musical director for a variety of television productions originating in Halifax and also performed locally. Eventually, he enlisted in the military and played saxophone with military bands before retiring to Dartmouth in 2003.

Penny MacAuley was a high school folksinger/songwriter in Halifax when she performed on the TV program *Round About* hosted by Frank Cameron. She auditioned for *Singalong* in 1970 and joined the show both as a solo and chorus singer. She was dubbed 'squeek' because of her soprano range. She performed as a backup singer for television, moved to Vancouver for a couple of years, then performed in clubs throughout the Maritimes until the mid-eighties. She moved into television production at ATV and at the CBC, directing mainly musical programming. She has done some independent production and is currently hosting and producing *Down East Café* for a community radio station in Eastern Passage. Penny organized the East Coast Music Industry Awards show in 2003, which included the tribute to Manny Pittson. She lives in Halifax.

Scott MacCulloch is from Bedford and was singing with the Scotia Male Chorale in the early 1960s when he joined the folk trio The Townsmen. They sang on *Singalong Jubilee* in 1963 then disbanded. Scott stayed in the chorus for another two years. He left *Singalong* in

1968 to join the family building supply business full time. Scott sings with the Bedford Chorale and has performed with the revived Townsmen for special occasions.

Mike (Red) MacDonald was living in Halifax, playing the bass fiddle with Don Warner's band, when he was invited to play on the pilot for *Singalong* hosted by Bill Langstroth. He performed regularly with *Singalong* for its first two seasons. Mike left the show due to job pressures with All State Insurance, then worked with the Department of Transportation. He retired recently from the Cape Breton Development Corporation.

Fred McKenna was a singer, guitarist and songwriter from Fredericton, educated at the Halifax School for the Blind. Blind from birth, he played the guitar, mandolin and fiddle on his lap, performing throughout the Maritimes. His television career began with guest appearances on *Don Messer's Jubilee* in 1958, and he then joined *Singalong Jubilee* as musical director, and regular solo and chorus performer from 1961. He moved to Toronto in 1968 but continued to perform on *Singalong* until 1973. Fred began recording for the Rodeo label in the 1950s and later made three LP's for *ARC* and one for *RCA*, some of which included his own compositions. Fred continued recording and performing until his death in 1977 at the age of 43.

Catherine McKinnon was born in Saint John, New Brunswick. She first appeared on radio on the local *Uncle Bill* show when she was seven, and on television on CFPL in London when she was nine. She joined *Singalong Jubilee* for the summer of 1963 both in the chorus and as a soloist, while still a music student at Mount Saint Vincent University in Halifax. Her first LP, *Voice of An Angel*, was an instant hit. She moved to Toronto in 1966 but continued to be a regular soloist on *Singalong* for the duration of the series and became a regular performer with *Don Messer's Jubilee*. After *Singalong*, Catherine also began doing musical theatre and acting. When not on the road, she divides her time between her homes on Prince Edward Island and in Toronto.

Patrician Anne McKinnon is the younger sister of Catherine McKinnon. She also performed from a young age and studied at Mount Saint Vincent Academy. She joined the *Singalong* chorus for the summer of 1964 at the age of 16 and stayed with the series for its duration. She moved to Toronto with Catherine in 1966. She co-hosted the final season of *Singalong* with Tom Kelly. Patrician Anne was diagnosed with Hodgkins disease in 1972. She passed away in 2000.

Gene MacLellan was born in Quebec and raised in Toronto, where he began a performing career with a rock band called Little Caesar and the Consuls in the early 1960s. He lived on Prince Edward Island from 1964 to 1977, and became a regular solo and chorus performer with *Singalong* in 1970. A songwriter, his most notable hits included *Snowbird* (the most frequently recorded Canadian song ever), and *Put Your Hand In the Hand*. The *Singalong* family dubbed him 'Whitey' for his preference for wearing white socks. Gene took his own life in 1995.

Gordon McMurtry was born in Saint John and grew up in the Annapolis Valley. He was always involved with music, singing *Gilbert and Sullivan*, with the Dal Glee Club, and with the Dal Law Quartet. He was one of the singers on the original pilot and joined the *Singalong* chorus in 1961. He was the tenor with The Jubilee Four and performed barber-shop harmonies on *Singalong* until the mid-sixties. He worked for Imperial Oil, then for Trust companies, continuing to sing until he died of cancer in 1988.

Robbie MacNeill is from Halifax. He joined *Singalong Jubilee* as a young guitarist for two seasons in the mid 1960s, then became musical director with The Privateers, a

PROFILES AND CREDITS

Halifax-based folk chorus. In 1968, he began touring with Anne Murray for several years before moving to Toronto. He spent the next 20 years touring with John Allan Cameron as his guitarist and musical director for a CTV television series. At this time, he also worked with the Toronto-based country-rock band, Albert Hall. Robbie began song writing in the late 60s. He now lives in South Branch, Nova Scotia, where he performs locally and continues his song writing.

Jim Michieli came to Toronto from England in 1953, having worked in wig-making, and began working in the CBC makeup department. In 1955, he joined CBC Halifax where he has worked ever since, except for a three-year sojourn back in Toronto from 1966 to 1969. He provided makeup for most of *Singalong Jubilee*'s run. Jim retired from the CBC in 1996 and lives in Halifax, but continues to do makeup as required.

Vern Moulton is from Halifax's North End. He was recruited to sing on the original *Singalong* pilot and stayed with the show for 10 years, both in the chorus and as a member of the trio The Dropouts. During the 1960s, Vern also sang with The Whi-Tones. Vern worked in the family shoe repair business, then in insurance, and finally in the wholesale business until he retired. He now lives in Lower Sackville and sings in the church choir.

Vic Mullen grew up in Yarmouth County, Nova Scotia, beginning his career in country music in 1949 with travelling bands. After guest spots on *Don Messer's Jubilee*, he became a regular from 1963 to 1969. For the 1966 to 1968 seasons, he also played banjo and twelve-string guitar on *Singalong*. He then became band leader and music director for *Country Time*, the CBC network television show based in Halifax, and hosted *Country Road*, the CBC radio network program. He retired to Port Maitland in 1997. He continues to teach music and perform occasionally.

Anne Murray is from Springhill, Nova Scotia. She was studying Physical Education at the University of New Brunswick in 1964 when she first auditioned for *Singalong*. She first appeared on the show in the summer of 1966, joining the cast and quickly becoming known across the country. In 1969, she released her first hit, *Snowbird*, and in 1971 she moved to Toronto. She occasionally made guest appearances on *Singalong* as she began her international recording and performing career. Anne married Bill Langstroth, host of *Singalong Jubilee*. She has released 33 albums, which have sold more than 50 million copies worldwide and won 31 Juno Awards, numerous other awards and is a Companion of the Order of Canada. Anne continues to record and perform.

Karen Oxley was a Haligonian who joined the *Jubilee Singers* in 1962 at the age of 16. She became a soloist, chorus leader and sound consultant on *Singalong*. She also appeared on other local CBC music programs such as *Music Hop, Frank's Bandstand, Let's Go* and *Countrytime*. She was a member of *The Dropouts*. Karen married drummer Jack Lilly. She was diagnosed with multiple sclerosis and died in 1992.

Manny Pittson was born in Halifax. He landed his first broadcasting job in 1955 while studying engineering at Dalhousie University. By 1960, he was producer and/or director for all kinds of general programming at CBC Halifax. He was the original producer of *Singalong Jubilee* from 1961 to 1973, except for the summers of 1967 and 1968. He also produced and directed *Frank's Bandstand* from 1964 to 1967. During the 1970s, he developed, produced and directed 500 half-hours of music programming, including *Don Messer's Jubilee* for CHCH in Hamilton. Manny joined the Media Arts Department of Sheridan College in Oakville, ON, in 1986, where he taught until his early retirement due to Parkinson's Disease in 1999. In 2003, the East Coast Music Awards honoured him with the Stompin' Tom Connors Award in recognition of his pioneering work in the development of music videos.

Garth Proude is originally from Charlottetown. He played with PEI's first rock 'n' roll group, the Tremtones, while still in high school, and was recruited by Brian Ahern in 1965 to become part of the house band for *Frank's Bandstand*. In 1966, he joined *Singalong Jubilee* and played bass with the house band, Musical Friends, for the duration of the series until 1974, becoming band leader from 1969. He joined Yamaha Canada Music in 1975 and continues to represent the company throughout the Maritimes. Garth continues to perform with Georges Hébert, Bucky Adams, Bill Stevenson, John Alphonse and many others.

Ted Regan is originally from Toronto and joined the CBC in Montreal in 1967 as a cameraman. Later, he worked as a director, and in 1973 he was appointed executive producer of Entertainment Programming for the Maritimes, responsible for all musical and variety network programming originating here. He was also director and producer for *Singalong Jubilee* in its final season. He left the CBC in 1979 to develop his own production company. In 1998 Ted settled in the Chester area, working with the Screen Arts program at the Nova Scotia Community College, and now works as a freelance director of documentaries.

Glen Reid is from Northern Ontario, a studio musician who performed with Fred McKenna in Toronto in the early seventies. Fred recruited him for *Singalong Jubilee* where he played banjo and rhythm guitar and performed a few of his own songs. After *Singalong* he lived in Halifax, travelling with the band The Ferriers until he returned to Toronto in the late seventies. He released three CDs, eventually returning to his home town and the family farm. These days, Glen builds guitars and mandolins in addition to teaching, writing, performing and recording music from Burk's Falls, outside North Bay.

Steve Rhymer is a Haligonian who began his musical career with Brian Ahern's rock 'n' roll group, The Badd Cedes, in the mid 1960s. He joined *Singalong* for the 1969 and 1970 seasons as a guitarist with the house band Musical Friends and as a chorus member. He sang the occasional solo. Steve also composed songs that were performed and recorded by Catherine McKinnon, Anne Murray, Emmylou Harris and others. In 1977, he moved to Port Wade on the Annapolis Basin, working a variety of jobs.

Antoinette (Toni) Roach / Hollett was encouraged by her piano teacher, Ray Calder, the original accordion and piano player on *Singalong*, to audition in 1961. She sang with the chorus from 1962 to 1970 while working at a finance company. She now works as an administrator for Greater Homes Realty, and lives in Dartmouth.

Michael Scott (see Howard Solverson)

Joe Sealy came to Halifax from Montreal in 1967 to play keyboard for *Frank's Bandstand*. That summer he became musical director for *Singalong*. He stayed in Halifax until 1976 as musical host for the daily CBC TV show *Round About* and performed locally before moving to Toronto, where he has been performing, acting and developing his company, Seajam Recordings.

Howard Solverson (known as Michael Scott) was born in Medicine Hat, Alberta, and joined the Canadian Navy after attending the University of Calgary. This brought him to Halifax in the late 1960s, where as singer/guitarist

PROFILES AND CREDITS

he led various folk groups, including the folk chorus The Privateers. In 1970, he was recruited to the *Singalong* chorus, where he also sang the occasional solo. He remained with *Singalong* until its demise, then returned to university and went to India as a volunteer. After extensive travel, back at university in Halifax in the early eighties, he performed with Karen Oxley and others at ATV, until he returned to international development work in Zimbabwe and Bhutan. These days, he divides his time between Canada and France.

Michael Stanbury was a Halifax high school student in the late 1950s when he caught the folk bug. A singer with the Scotian Male Choral, he co-founded The Townsmen in 1962. They had a regular spot on *Singalong Jubilee* for the summer of 1963 and then disbanded. Michael studied acting and worked as a performer in Montreal and Toronto until 1969 when he returned to *Singalong Jubilee* and became musical director until 1971. Michael then obtained a diploma in engineering technology and works as a design technologist in Halifax.

Bob Theakston joined the CBC in Halifax as a sound technician in radio in 1954, moving to television in 1955. Bob worked as sound engineer for *Singalong Jubilee* for virtually all of its 13 years and was also responsible for the sound on the *Singalong Jubilee* LPs. He retired in 1987 as technical manager and lives on Nova Scotia's South Shore.

Ken Tobias is originally from Saint John, New Brunswick, where he formed a folk-bluegrass group The Ramblers with his brother. Ken moved to Halifax to perform on *Frank's Bandstand*, and was also part of a rock 'n' roll group the Badd Cedes. He joined *Singalong* for 1965 to 1967 as guitarist, solo then chorus performer. Ken then moved to Montreal, and to Los Angeles, where he recorded his first hit *You're Not Even Going to the Fair* with Bill Medley of the Righteous Brothers. He has recorded two albums, and his best known hit is *Stay Awhile* recorded by The Bells. He moved to Toronto in 1972, where he continues to perform and record albums, write music for films, television, commercials and a ballet. In the past two decades, Ken has become a painter.

Sylvia Wedderburn was born in New York City and came to Halifax in 1959 working as a nurse at the Victoria General Hospital. She was recruited by Bill Langstroth in 1961 to join the *Singalong* chorus. Being of West Indian background, she also sang a few calypso solos in her two years on the show. Over the years, she has sung with the Atlantic Symphony Choir, the Dal Chorale, the Chebucto Community Singers and the Aeolian Singers.

Davey Wells was nick-named 'Uppey' because his real family name was Upshaw. From Halifax, Davey began his performing career on CBC Halifax's *Frank's Bandstand* in 1964. He joined *Singalong* in 1967 as both a solo and chorus performer. He continued performing in and around the Maritimes with the Musical Friends and also with the Four Winds. Davey moved to Toronto in the mid-seventies and worked as a performer. In 1980, he returned to Halifax and worked as a commissionaire, while continuing to perform when the opportunity arose. He died of cancer in January 2002.

Lorne White was number 12 of a famous musical family of 13, growing up in the North End of Halifax in the 1930s. He was teaching physical education and singing at

REMEMBERING SINGALONG JUBILEE

any invitation when Bill Langstroth recruited him to sing on the original *Singalong* pilot. Lorne continued singing with the chorus for 13 seasons, with the Jubilee Four, with the Dropouts, and as a soloist doing spirituals and blues numbers. Lorne retired from teaching in 1986 and continues to perform for special occasions and fundraising events as well as being a regular with his church choir.

PERFORMING CREDITS

Harry Boss
Noah Boutlier
Dave Bradstreet
Garth Brown
George Buckley
Ray Calder
Lisa Dal Bella
Earl Fralick

Joan Forsham
Lennie Gallant
Cynthia Griffin
Dianne Gunn
Jack Harris
Don Harron
Harry Hibbs
Dee Higgins

Peggy Mahon
Sandy MacDonald
Fran MacMillan
Kay MacMillan
Alan Mills
Kay Porter
Betty Rice
Ryan's Fancy

Jim Sears
Bud Spencer
Elan Stuart
Joyce Sullivan
Brent Titcomb
Hazel Walker
Nancy White

PRODUCTION CREDITS

Chris Adeney
Caroline Aldred
Rolf Blei
Robert Blom
Doug Beattie
Jack Brennen
Maureen Britton
Don Brown
Jack Brownell
Harold Buckley
Bill Campbell
Keith Campbell
Joey Carver
Paul Cormer
Terry Crocker
Vonda Crozier
Ed Curtis
Doug Dauphinee

Steve Delory
Dave Dixon
Kate Elliott
George Elrick
Bernie Fletcher
Ray Fralick
Terry Fullmer
Gerry Gagnon
Ross Gardner
Roger Gentleman
Jack Goodhew
Bill Grice
Arnold Hubley
John Huskins
Don Jackson
Athan Katsos
Chuck Latter
Garry Langille

Penny Longley
Sandra Marshall
Ann Martin
Fred Martin
John Martin
Bob Mason
Kent MacDonald
Al Macpherson
Peter McNeil
Gordy MacNeil
Dave McClafferty
Curt McSwain
Dave Morrison
Frank Myers
Hazel Oliver
Jack O'Neil
Gary Oxner
Dorothy Payne

Clary Phillips
Gerry Roach
Marty Raine
Joe Ratto
Charlie Reynolds
Don Ring
Mickie Ryan
Glen Sarty
Stan Scallion
Paul Scott
Herbert Skinner
Bob Smith
Jim Snow
Winston Teal
Cy True
Gerry Wile
Christine Zinck

INDEX

ABC Hootenannies 16
Adeney, Chris 12
Aeolian Singers 85, 93
Ahern, Brian 28, 29, 45, 66-69, 85
Alexander, Audrey 7, 18-19, 85
Alf Coward Show 25
Alibi Room 25
AM Chronicle 10
Anthes, Tom 85
Armdale Chorus 89
art, album covers 40, 56, 82, 83
"As Good as it Got" 5
Ashcroft, Marg 17, 63, 79, 84, 85
   enjoying singing 43, 69
   family bonds 43, 54
audience
   demographics 40, 74, 75, 81
   numbers 39-40, 74, 75, 81, 83
   ratings 8, 14, 40, 60-61, 69, 75
   response 8, 39-40, 74, 75, 81
Audrey and Alex 7, 85

The Badd Cedes 92, 93
Baylis, Paul 85
Beals, Gary 83
Bennet, Jim 7, 11, 14, 16, 25, 46-47, 85
   host 13, 15, 25
Big Bopper 31
Black Rum and Blueberry Pie 46-47
Brickenden, Fred 'Brick' 10-12
broadcasts. *See also* locations
   Christmas 25, 26, 37, 50, 51, 77, 83
   Remembrance 76, 80
   10th Anniversary 70, 73, 74
Brockner, Martin 14
Brown, Clarke 80, 84
The Brunswick Playboys 22
Bunkhouse Boys 22, 88
Burke, Betty-Anne 21
Burke, Don 11, 24, 38, 67, 68, 86
Butler, Edith 7, 44-45, 61, 86

Calder, Ray 92
The Call 7, 69
Calloway, Cab 33
Cameron, John Allan 7, 36, 37, 86
Carr, David 25, 86
cast 6, 55, 69, 83. *See also Singalong Jubilee*
   changes in 73, 75, 77, 78
   illustrations of 8, 11, 22, 26, 55, 84
   'in the round' 10, 13, 36
   key members 11, 24, 32, 50, 57-72
CBC 25, 39-40, 51-52
   dropping Pete Seeger 12-13
   'Halifax Sound' 27, 29, 67
   program development 29-30, 60-61, 73-82
   'right-Toronto' 73-82
CBHT (CBC) 25, 75, 76, 88
Chantilly Lace 31
Chebucto Community Singers 85, 93
The Cherry Tree Carol 15
Citadel Hill mobile 72
Connor, Blake 86
Cormier, J.P. 83
country music 61, 64, 65
Creighton, Helen 8, 15, 25, 37, 83

Croft, Clary 42, 46-47, 86
   beginnings 7, 22-23, 25, 59
   collection of songs 83, 86
   on program changes 77, 80
Crush 83

Davidson, George 39
Davies-MacDonald, Marilyn 11, 68, 86
Day, Graham 17, 55, 58-59, 60, 86-87
Degens, Louise 12
deLong, Nancy 84
D'Eon, Geoff 5
Diamond Trio 11, 36
Ditchburn, Anne 78-79
Doane, Chalmers 64, 65-66, 87
Doane, Herb 87
Dodge, Ron 87
Don Burke Four 68, 85, 86
Don Messer's Jubilee 53, 69, 88, 91
   cancellation 39-40, 81-83
   replaced by *Singalong* 9-10, 40
   style 32-33, 60
Downeasters 25
Dropouts 56, 65, 66, 91, 94

East Coast Music Industry Awards 83, 89, 91
Eikhard, Shirley 7, 23-24, 59-60, 77, 87
episodes
   Christmas broadcasts 25, 26, 37, 50, 51, 77, 83
   Remembrance Day show 76, 80
   10th Anniversary Broadcast 70, 73, 74
Every Bit of Love 7

Face in the Mirror 7
Farewell to Nova Scotia 7-8
Flynn, Teddy 52, 87
Fogarty, Eva 52, 85
folk culture 8, 10, 15
folk music 8, 10, 66-67, 82
   Maritime 7-8, 14, 15, 25, 35, 37, 83, 86
Folksong Jubilee 9, 57
Four Winds 89, 93
Frank's Bandstand 15, 22, 29, 35, 66-67, 91

Gallant-Bona, Jeanette (Jay) 87
'gold dust twins' 23
Gorsebrook Research Institute 5-6
Great Speckled Bird 88, 89
Greenwood mobile 31, 49
Greer, Al 87-88
Grice, Bill 34
Grigsby, Wayne 49, 51, 58, 78, 82-83, 88
Guess Who 84

'Halifax Sound' 27, 29, 67
Harper, Bill 5
Harris, Jackie 69
Hébert, Georges 29, 53, 71, 81, 88
   beginnings 22
   family bonds 43
   sound production 29-30
Hi-Society 25

Hibbs, Harry 7
Highwaymen On Tour 16
Homer, Ken 25
Hurford, Sandy 80, 84
Hymn Sing 76, 77

I Just Want to Make Music 7
In the Early Morning Rain 34
'in the round' 10, 13, 36
Isnor, Milt 30-31, 46, 52, 63, 88
It Takes Time 7, 60, 87

Jackson, Don 30
Jubilee Four 87, 88, 90, 94
Jubilee Singers 13, 15, 76. *See also* cast; *Singalong Jubilee*
Jubilee Years 5, 89
Just Bidin' My Time 7, 70

Kelly, Tom 38, 76, 79, 80, 84, 88
   co-host 38, 43-44, 73
   on program changes 38-39, 77
Kempster, Hal 7, 44, 52, 61, 69, 84, 88
   'Poppa' 41-42
Kennedy, Syd 10-11
Kimball, Bud 88

Laird, Arthur 75-76
Land of Old Songs 25
Langstroth, Bill 47, 71-72, 88-89
   family bonds 54-56
   host 7, 13-16, 71-72
   illustrations of 11-14, 19, 37, 45, 47
   performer 13, 71-72, 75
   producer 10, 20, 37, 62
   retirement 73, 82-83
   upbeat character 45, 71-72
Lilly, Jack 22, 52, 64, 84, 89
   beginnings 22, 67
   family bonds 49, 52, 64
Limelighter 16
lip-synching 27-28, 34
locations 13, 34, 60
   Citadel Hill mobile 72
   Greenwood 31, 49
   'old mill' set 55, 67
   St. Paul's Anglican Church 34-35
   Tatamagouche 34, 35
   Uniacke House 42, 83
Longley, Penny 37, 89
Lumsden, Sandy 75, 76

MacAndrew, Jack 19-20, 54, 71
MacAuley, Penny 7, 22, 23, 41, 54-55, 89
MacCulloch, Scott 89-90
MacDonald, Mike (Red) 90
MacIsaac, Ashley 83
MacLellan, Gene 34, 49, 53-54, 64, 90
   beginnings 7
   sense of humour 45-46
   talent 69-71
MacMaster, Natalie 83
MacNeil, Rita 83
MacNeill, Robbie 7, 22, 90-91
Mahone, Peggy 27
Mariposa Festival 16
Maritime folk culture 47, 74, 80-81, 84

folk music 7-8, 14, 15, 25, 35, 37, 83, 86
folklore 8, 86
Martin, Sharon 89
Mason, Paul 89
Massey Ferguson 10, 39
Matthews, Thomas 30
McClafferty, Dave 63
McKenna, Fred 11, 47-52, 61-65, 90
   beginnings 7, 13
   and program changes 73, 78
   retirement 73
   talent 13, 15, 29
McKinnon, Catherine 11, 21, 33, 57, 78-79, 90
   beginnings 7-8, 15-17, 25, 59
   family bonds 42-43, 46, 48
   talent 15, 65-66
McKinnon, Patrician Anne 21, 23, 33-34, 79, 84, 90
   beginnings 7, 21
   family bonds 48, 52, 54
   illness 52-53
   talent 23, 42
McMurtry, Gordon 52, 90
Melva (Fred McKenna's wife) 50-51, 62
Messer, Don 10, 14, 22, 82
Michieli, Jim 49, 53, 91
Miller, Mitch 10
mobiles (location shoots) 31-34, 60, 72, 86
   Citadel Hill mobile 72
   Greenwood 31, 49
   'old mill' set 55, 67
Moulton, Vern 8, 56, 65, 66, 91
Moving Images of Nova Scotia 6
MuchMusic 34
Mullen, Vic 91
Murray, Anne 18, 31, 49, 65, 70-71, 76, 91
   beginnings 7, 19-20, 71
   family bonds 44, 46, 52, 54-56
   recording 60-61, 69, 70, 83, 91
   talent 42, 60, 69, 91
Murray, David 19
Music Hop 15, 21, 22, 84, 91
music
   country music 61, 64, 65
   folk music 8, 10, 66-67, 82
   Maritime folk music 7-8, 14, 15, 25, 35, 37, 83, 86
   popular music 38
   videos 7, 31-34
music, developments 27-31, 68-69
Musical Friends 8, 89, 92, 93

Nelson, Ricky 31
Nixon, Doug 39
North Country Fair 34

O'Neil, Jack 11-13, 60-61
Ottawa Citizen 15
Oxley, Karen 45, 78, 91
   beginnings 7, 17-18, 25
   family bonds 41-42, 53
   illustrations of 34, 46, 48, 56, 61, 80, 84

talent 41-42, 44, 65-66

Peter Emberly 78-79
Pittson, Manny 12, 7-8, 30, 57-61, 91-92
   contract dropped 73, 78, 81
   honoured 89, 91
   mentor 5, 44
   producer 13, 15, 27-28, 32-34, 37, 43, 57-61, 89
Poor Little Girls of Ontar-i-o 66
Porter, Kay 68
The Privateers 86, 87, 90, 92-93
Proude, Garth 30, 46, 49, 53, 69, 92
   beginnings 22, 64, 67
   family bonds 49
   recording 30
Put Your Hand in the Hand 7, 69-70, 90

The Ramblers 21, 93
The Rankins 83
Reflections 25
Regan, Ted 73-81, 85
Reid, Glen 92
Reid, Johnny 23
Remembrance Day episode 76, 80

Rhymer, Steve 7, 67, 92
Roach/Hollett, Antoinette (Toni) 8, 26, 92
Robbie's Song for Jesus 7
Ryan's Fancy 79

St. Paul's Anglican Church 34-35
Sarty, Glen 5, 10-12
Scotia Male Chorale 87, 89, 93
Scott, Michael. *See* Howard Solverson
Sealy, Joe 92
Seeger, Pete 9-13, 36
Singalong Jubilee
   auditions 16-24, 37-38
   cancellation 40, 76, 79, 81, 82
   careers launched 7, 20-21, 73, 83
   changes 73, 75-81
   early history 7, 9-13, 25-31
   excellence 7, 14-15, 27, 35, 73-74, 77, 82-84
   family bonds 41-56, 78
   music videos 7, 31-34
   production 25-31, 43-45, 60-61
   professionalism 35-38, 73-74
   ratings 8, 14, 40, 60-61, 69, 74-76, 81
   reviews 14-15, 38, 40, 61, 73-74

title 10, 13
Singalong with Mitch Miller 10, 11
singing 'in the round' 10, 13, 36
Skelton, Red 72
Smith, Bob 30
Snowbird 7, 60, 69, 70, 90, 91
Solverson, Howard (a.k.a. Michael Scott) 78, 84, 92-93
Sophie's 42
Stanbury, Michael 8, 24, 17, 50, 93
Starmer, Len 51-52
Stay Awhile 7, 93
Stuart, Elan 13, 15, 16, 47, 62
Studio One 26, 86

Teddy Bear's Picnic 34
television 7, 60-61
   Canadian 7, 10, 13
   early technology 25-31, 36
Thanks A Lot For the Teabag 46
Theakston, Bob 28, 29-30, 93
Then Again 5
Thorn in My Shoe 7
Tobias, Ken 8, 34, 63, 67-68, 93
   beginnings 7, 21
   family bonds 44, 50-51
Tommy Hunter 76, 78

Toronto Daily Star 40
Townsmen 28, 86, 89, 90, 93
Travelin' Man 31
The Tremtones 22, 92

Uniacke House 42, 83

Vaughan, Alex 85
video 25
videos, music 7, 31-34, 92
The Voice of an Angel 61, 90
Wedderburn, Sylvia 19, 93
Weekend Magazine 35, 61, 74
Wells, Davey 45, 46, 52-53, 64, 93
   beginnings 21-22
   family bonds 43, 49, 53
White, Lorne 35, 53, 66, 93-94
   illustrations of 7, 48, 54, 56, 61, 65
Willis, J. Frank 46

You're Not Even Going to the Fair 93

Znaimer, Moses 34

SOURCES

Page 13: We're Like a Family – A Happy Family in *Weekend Magazine*, 15 January 1972
Page 14: Bob Sheils – *Herald Magazine,* 29 July 1961; Marion Lepkin – *Winnipeg Free Press,* 8 July 1961; Martin Brockner (Concert Promoter): letter to Manny Pittson, 18 July 1961; Pat Pearce – *Montreal Star,* 10 July 1962
Page 15: Andrew Webster - *Ottawa Citizen,* 7 August 1962; Helen Creighton. Letter to Manny Pittson, 18 September 1963; Bob Burgess – *Ottawa Citizen,* 18 September 1962
Page 16: Elan Stewart, *Jubilee Years,* 13 March 1993
Page 17: Marg Ashcroft, *Jubilee Years,* 17 May 1994; Michael Stanbury, *Jubilee Years,* 20 March 1993; Karen Oxley, *Jubilee Years,* 6 February 1993
Page 18: Karen Oxley / Interview with Tom Gallant 1973
Page 20: Anne Murray, *Jubilee Years,* 21 May 1994
Page 21: *Jubilee Years,* 20 February 1993; Ken Tobias, *Jubilee Years,* 25 June 1994; Davey Wells *Jubilee Years,* 16 April 1994
Page 22: Garth Proude, *Jubilee Years,* 27 Aug 1994; Jack Lilly, *Jubilee Years,* 27 Aug 1994; George Hebert, *Jubilee Years,* 27 Aug 1994
Page 23: Shirley Eikhard, *Jubilee Years,* no date
Page 33: Manny Pittson (top) *Jubilee Years,* 27 March 1993; Manny Pittson (bottom) *Then Again* 1996-97; Catherine McKinnon, *Jubilee Years,* 9 Janury 1993; Patrician Ann McKinnon, *Jubilee Years,* 20 February 1993
Page 34: Bill Langstroth *Then Again* 1996-97

Page 35: *Weekend Magazine* #18 1965
Page 38: *Maclean's*, 1966; *Nova Scotia Magazine* 1970
Page 40: Patrick Scott, *Toronto Daily Star,* 16 April 1969
Page 43: Davey Wells, *Jubilee Years,* 16 April 1994
Page 44: Anne Murray, *Jubilee Years,* 2 January 1993; Hal Kempster, *Jubilee Years,* 17 May 1994; Ken Tobias 25 June 1994; Edith Butler, *Jubilee Years,* 14 November 1992
Page 56: Vern Moulton, *Jubilee Years,* 6 February 1993
Page 61: *Weekend Magazine* 15 January 1972
Page 62: Hal Kempster, *Jubilee Years,* 6 August 1994; Elan Stewart, *Jabilee Years,* 13 March 1993
Page 63: Marg Ashcroft 6 August 1994; Ken Tobias, *Jubilee Years,* 6 August 1994
Page 64: Gene MacLellan, *Jubilee Years,* 6 August 1994; Davey Wells, *Jubilee Years,* 6 August 1994; Garth Proude 6 August 1994
Page 65: Anne Murray, *Jubilee Years,* 2 January 1993
Page 66: Karen Oxley interview with Tom Gallant, 1973
Page 67 and 69: Brian Ahern, *Jubilee Years,* 11 June 1994
Page 70: Gene Maclellan, *Jubilee Years,* 5 December 1992
Page 71: Jack MacAndrew, *Then Again* 1996-97
Page 73: Interview with Fred McKenna, (Richard Green c. 1975)
Page 73-4: *Weekend Magazine* 15 January 1972
Page 75-76: Arthur Laird, Director of Audience Research
Page 77: Canadian Broadcasting Corporation, press release 19 September 1973